Clean Eating Cookbook for Beginners

including guidelines and over 100

healthy recipes to eating clean

following the correct way

By Courtney Fox

tips, advice, counsel, strategies and techniques that may be offered in this volume.

Table of Contents

Introduction

Congratulations on purchasing Clean Eating Cookbook for Beginners: The Complete Clean Eating Book with Over 100 Healthy, Whole-Food Recipes for Instant, Overnight, and Easy Comfort Foods. Easy Keto, Low-Carb, Vegetarian, and Vegan Cookbook and Healthy Recipes for Weight Loss Diet by Courtney Fox and thank you for doing so.

The following chapters will discuss the idea of clean eating and what it can do for you. Decades ago, people didn't pay much attention to the food they ate, as long as it tasted good. A sugary dessert was the perfect end to a great meal. Soft drinks and snacks were available whenever you wanted them. No one worried about weight gain or trans fats or any of the millions of other food-related concerns that keep us awake at night. They were too busy carrying on with their lives to need to worry.

But as the people of the world became more sedentary, as modern conveniences made our lives easier, food became more of an afterthought. Mindless eating became the norm. The world of conveniences spilled over into our food, too. Meals were easy to grab on the run, meals full of excess fats and sugars, and all sorts of chemicals that no one's body needs.

Enter the idea of clean eating. It isn't so strange after all, because it is the way people ate decades ago when they could still enjoy the occasional soft drink and slice of cake. Back then, people ate cleanly; they prepared meals and snacks that were created from real food, raw food, fresh food that they bought, and brought home and made delicious meals from. And they were healthy. And you will be healthy, too, once you make the decision to adopt the idea of clean eating for yourself.

This book will give you the information that you need to know about clean eating, from what it is to who will benefit from it the most. You will learn easy ways to eat cleanly. And there are recipes, over one hundred delicious recipes made from real food, recipes for keto eating plans and vegetarians and low carb eaters and vegans. No matter your style of eating, this book has what you need to succeed in a clean food eating style.

There are plenty of books on this subject on the market, thanks again for choosing this one! Every effort was made to ensure it is full of as much useful information as possible, please enjoy!

Chapter 1: What Is Clean Eating?

Clean eating is just exactly what it says it is – clean eating. The very basis of clean eating is to select foods and drinks that are kept as close to their natural state as they can possibly be. You will choose foods that are fresh and whole instead of sugary treats, processed foods, and pre-packaged foods. You will consume a diet that is made of vegetables, fruits, lean proteins, whole grains, legumes, seeds, nuts, and healthy fats, which are all of the foods that your body needs to be healthy and happy. You will limit processed foods, sugary foods and drinks, pre-packaged foods, and any other food or drink that is full of calories with very few nutrients.

You will also want to avoid foods and drinks that are altered drastically from their natural form. This means that you will eat the apple or the orange instead of drinking the juice. You will eat a chicken breast purchased fresh instead of the chicken nuggets from the local drive-thru restaurant. The fruits and veggies you choose to eat will be in their fresh state and not made into chips or dried into leather. Some processing is allowed, since the process of pasteurization makes dairy products and eggs safe for you to consume. Veggies and fruits that are picked at the peak of their season and quickly frozen are also allowed, since they will have the same nutrients as the fresh varieties and they are usually processed very minimally. You will also want to avoid added chemicals and preservatives in your food.

Your meals will be prepared mostly at home so that you can choose the foods that you will eat and prepare them for your liking. You do have room for some flexibility, and you do not need to avoid any particular foods or food groups unless you have a medical necessity, like celiac disease, or if you choose to avoid certain foods. You can eat clean on any diet style, which includes keto, low-carb, vegetarian, or vegan.

The Benefits of Clean Eating

Foods that are unprocessed include farm-fresh eggs, nuts, seeds, dried legumes, and fresh veggies, and fruits. Foods that are minimally processed include healthy oils, dairy that is free from hormones, meat that is free form hormones and preferably raised in a pasture and not raised on grain for feeding, frozen veggies and fruits, and grains that have not been refined like brown rice, quinoa, steel-cut oatmeal, popcorn, and whole-wheat pasta and bread.

Foods that are free of pesticides are preferred so you are not consuming any added chemicals or hormones. And eating clean does not mean eating as much as you want of any food that you wish to, because clean food still contains calories. You will not need to eat all of your food raw, but you do need to stick to minimal processing. Always shop around the perimeter of the store first and get most of your meals from there.

Cooking your food does alter it somewhat, but this processing can be good for your food. While some vitamins might be lost in cooking others will find their potency increased. The best way to eat clean is to consume a mixture of raw foods and minimally cooked foods so that you collect all of your nutrients. The challenge is to maintain the integrity of the food as close as you can, so while foods might be cooked, they should not be stewed or fried in vegetables or animal fats. The best ways to cook your foods are steaming or stir-frying, and slow-cooking or baking is also an option if the food is not coated with extra fats.

So what can a diet of clean eating do for you? Plenty, if you let it. When you choose to eat a diet of foods that are clean and whole then you will be filling your body with the nutrients you need to be healthy and resist disease. Each of the food groups has their own ability to keep you healthy.

WHOLE GRAINS – When you fill your diet with refined carbs like white rice, white bread, and white pasta, you are simply eating calories to fill your belly. These foods have been so stripped of their nutrients during the refining process that they are little more than plates full of empty calories. When you choose wild rice, brown rice, whole-wheat pasta, and whole-grain bread, then you are choosing foods that are full of good nutrition. Add in other healthy grains like bulgur, barley, popcorn, and oatmeal to really round out your menu options. When your diet that is full of whole grains, you can dramatically decrease the risk that you will develop colon cancer, type 2 diabetes, and heart disease.

VEGGIES AND FRUITS – These are two staples of the clean eating diet because they are purely natural foods. Depending on your lifestyle, you will need to eat between five and nine servings of fruits and veggies every day. And remember that the whole fruit is much better for you than the juice. Canned and frozen options can be used as fill-ins for the fresh choices since they will not spoil as quickly, and they are just as healthy for you. Just read the nutrition label to make sure there are no added sugars, salts, or preservatives and chemicals.

ADDED SUGAR AND SALT – When you eat clean foods, you will be eating foods that are naturally low in sugar and salt. Adding these two items to your foods goes against the clean eating idea of eating foods in a state that is as close to natural as possible. When you remove the processed foods from your diet, you will be removing a major source of added sugar and salt. You will also need to read the nutritional labels on any 'healthy' food that you buy because even healthy foods like tomato sauce and yogurt can have added amounts of salt and sugar, along with other chemicals that you do not want to eat. Herbs and spices will become your new best friends for cooking.

ARTIFICIAL INGREDIENTS – Again, you will need to read your nutritional labels and look for foods without added chemicals and artificial ingredients that are made by man and not found in nature. Or only buy foods that are sold without labels like fresh meats, fish, fruits, and veggies.

DRINK WATER CONSTANTLY – This is not to say you can't have your morning coffee; after all, it is made with water. But the caffeine will dehydrate you, and water is still the best drink around. Stay away from fruit drinks, fruit juices, soft drinks, and energy drinks, because even the sugar-free ones are loaded with chemicals that you do not want to consume. The substance that makes a drink sugar free is a chemical in most cases. Plain water will hydrate you, energize you, and help to curb those cravings for foods. If you find that you really miss the taste of flavor in your water try infused waters by dropping in slices of veggies, fruits, or sprigs of mint.

LIMIT CAFFEINE AND ALCOHOL – Whether you completely eliminate them or only have them in moderation, keep in mind that caffeine and alcohol are made from chemicals that you do not really want in your clean eating regimen. Try to keep your coffee intake to five cups or less per day (which is still quite a bit!) and no more than one alcoholic beverage per day. And keep your tea or coffee plain and don't use the sweet mixers for the alcohol.

ORGANIC OR NOT – This decision is totally yours to make, and you will likely hear from both sides of the argument. Organic farmers avoid man-made pesticides in favor of natural ways to keep their plants safe from insects. If you do your shopping at a local farmer's market, you can always ask what pesticides those farmers use on their crops. But even if you choose not to go organic in your purchases, which can be a bit expensive at times, choose the non-organic options that have thick natural coverings like onions, cob corn, and avocadoes, skin that you will just peel off and throw away.

CHOOSE DAIRY AND MEAT WISELY – The eggs, dairy products, and meat that you buy from the store quite possible are made from animals that are filled with antibiotics and growth hormones. People who eat clean choose animal products that are free from these added chemicals. You can purchase only the organic options or source these foods from local options that raise their animals humanely. When purchasing seafood, there will be no organic labels, but you will look for fish and seafood that has a low mercury content and is sourced from vendors that use sustainable fishing. Or you can always get your protein from legumes, seeds, and nuts.

The Perils of Processed Foods

The term 'processed foods' includes any food that falls into one of the following categories:

- Any form of cooking is considered to be processing the food, even though this is a minimal method and not one to worry about.

- Any food that has ingredients that were created in a laboratory. If you are reading the list of ingredients and you see something that you can't pronounce or don't recognize, that is probably something that you don't want to eat. Those additives do not belong in your food, and those foods are not natural.

- Any time the food is changed drastically from its natural form to create another form of the food, like removing the germ and the bran from whole grains to make them into refined grains.

- Anytime preservatives are added to food to keep them from spoiling, or minerals and vitamins are used to enrich refined food.

Not all processing is bad. For example, milk is processed so that it will be safe to drink. When you toss bananas, kale, celery, and spinach into a blender to make a smoothie, you are processing those foods and altering their natural state. The processing that does not fit in with clean eating is the processing that creates a food item out of chemicals or foods that are created to be ready to eat or able to eat with minimal preparation.

There are many health problems that have been associated with foods that are highly processed. Those foods that have been genetically modified have been linked to a higher incidence of infertility and cancer. The nutrients that you need for your good health have been stripped out of foods that are highly processed. Many foods that are highly processed are full of chemicals that activate the production of the hormone dopamine in your brain. This hormone is often called the 'feel-good' hormone because it causes people to relax and feel good. This is why highly processed foods make you feel so good when you eat them.

Macros and Micros

No matter which food plan you choose to adopt while you are eating clean, you will most likely hear about macros and micros. You might choose to follow the keto diet, a low-carb diet, or a vegetarian or vegan diet, and there will be those people who will insist that you need to track your macros and be mindful of your micros if you intend to live a healthy life. Macros and micros are ways to identify the two different types of nutrients that your body needs, nutrients that you will get from the food that you consume.

Macronutrients (macros) are the three main food types that you will be eating, the fats, carbs, and proteins. Macros are the foods that you will need to eat in large quantities so that your body will have energy and the fuel it needs to function correctly. Micronutrients (micros) are the minerals, vitamins, phytochemicals, and antioxidants that your body needs to get from the food that you consume so that it can function properly. You will need micros in small quantities since they are involved in every process that your body does, from preventing diseases to digestion to the functioning of your immune system.

So the question remains, should you track your macros? This process might be beneficial for you if you are trying to reach a particular goal, like losing weight or building muscle, since each of these pursuits will require a different intake of fats, carbs, and proteins. When you track your macros, you can focus of a specific health goal by creating a balance of the macros that are tailored to your particular needs. By tracking your macros, you will be able to see what you are really eating and make adjustments to your diet if needed. But if you are eating a healthy mix of all of the macros, then you might not feel the need to track your macros. And if you are eating a well-balanced diet, then you will not need to track your micros because you will be getting all of the nutrients that you need from the food you eat.

Eating clean is not a difficult way to live, and when you make the decision to do it you will feel so much better physically and mentally. Clean eating will aid every part of your body and your mind. There are so many benefits to your health when you eating clean that you will wonder why you waited so long to begin. Packaged foods and processed foods are full of so many harmful additives that your body just does not need. They are full of preservatives, sugars, and toxins that will lead to a decreased immune system, healthy conditions, low energy, and obesity. You will improve your happiness, your weight, and your overall health by embracing the clean eating lifestyle.

Chapter 2: Who Will Benefit From Clean Eating?

Eating a diet full of clean food is the easiest way to lose weight and improve your health. When you make the commitment to eating a diet that is full of food free from toxins, you will see the benefits like better sleep habits, clearer skin, and weight loss. And eating fewer junk foods and more whole foods will help you to minimize the effects of chronic illnesses that you might already be suffering from and reduce the risk that you will develop others. When you eat clean, you will focus on lean meats, vegetables, fruits, nuts, seeds, and fish and eliminate refined foods and processed foods. There are definitely some essential benefits to committing to a lifestyle of clean dietary habits.

EATING CLEAN WILL MAKE YOUR SKIN CLEARER AND YOU HAPPIER. When the foods that you eat are right for you, then you will be consuming antioxidants and healthy fats that will give you glowing, beautiful skin. It will also help your skin to remain resilient and robust. Processed foods that are loaded with sodium and trans fats they can cause your skin to overproduce a substance known as sebum, which is responsible for keeping your skin hydrated. Too much sebum production will cause your pores to clog with oil and accumulated dirt, and this might lead to you developing acne. Clean foods contain phytochemicals that will combat the free radicals that can damage your skin. Fresh, whole foods also contain nutrients that feed your skin and your hair. And healthy foods have a positive effect on the hormones that your body secretes, particularly the happy hormones that your brain produces that help to keep your moods stable.

EATING CLEAN WILL ENERGIZE YOUR IMMUNE SYSTEM AND BOOST YOUR ENERGY LEVELS. When you feed your body on the phytochemicals, antioxidants, minerals, and vitamins in clean foods, then you will be providing a powerful natural boost to your immune system. These powerful nutrients work to stop inflammation and damage to your cells by creating the white blood cells that are the first line of defense for your body against diseases. When your immune system is healthy, it will be able to fight off infections and diseases, and you will be able to recover more quickly when you do get sick. And eating clean will help to boost your levels of energy and help you avoid that mid-afternoon energy slump. When you depend on processed carbs like sweets and cakes to give you energy, they will for a while because of the spike in blood sugar that these foods cause. But you will eventually feel the crash as the blood sugar levels back out or even drops lower than it was before. Relying on lean proteins and foods rich in fiber will give your body a more consistent source of energy that will balance your energy levels and give you what you need to get through the day.

EATING CLEAN WILL RESULT IN WEIGHT LOSS. So many people today are obese, and that obesity is a health condition that is associated with other health conditions like many types of cancer, heart disease, stroke, and type 2 diabetes. When switching to a diet of clean food, most people will find that they quickly lose weight. Even if you eat more often and eat more food when eating clean foods, the foods you are eating are so full of nutrients that you will be consuming fewer calories than before. And this type of diet will help you to curb those annoying cravings for junk food while it works to speed up your metabolism, and these will allow you to be able to lose weight effortlessly without feeling deprived or hungry. By eliminating or preventing obesity, then you will also be preventing or reversing a whole host of other chronic illnesses. And you will not be eating a diet that is full of chemicals, sugar, artificial sweeteners, and preservatives.

EATING CLEAN WILL HELP TO REDUCE INFLAMMATION. Your body needs some level of inflammation to provide protection to your body and respond to injuries or illnesses. But the chronic inflammation that comes from a diet high in toxins like trans fats and sugars and being overweight will put your body in a constant state of heightened levels of inflammation. A diet full of toxins has been known to increase the risk that you might develop certain forms of cancer, osteoporosis, high blood pressure, heart disease, diabetes, and arthritis. And just like excessive inflammation is promoted by a diet that is high in sugar, salt, trans fats, and other toxins, the inflammation will be reduced or eliminated by a diet that is made up of clean whole food.

Men and Women

Men have more muscles than women do, and they are usually bigger in size, so they will require a higher intake of calories during an average day than women will. Men who are only moderately active will require between two thousand two hundred calories and two thousand eight hundred calories every day just to sustain life. The calorie needs will depend on a man's activity level as well as his weight and height. Men need to load up on fruits and veggies along with whole grains like lentils, beans, barley, oats, brown rice, and whole-grain cereal, pasta, and bread. These foods will help a man to manage his hunger and keep himself full, and they will also help to guard against certain cancers like cancer of the colon or cancer of the prostate. Men should also get their protein from a variety of sources that include plant-based sources and fish and seafood. Stay away from full-fat dairy and meats that are full of fat. Fill your menu plans with fats that are good for your heart like avocados, seeds, nuts, canola oil, and olive oil.

Women should also embrace the benefits that they will get from eating a clean diet, but for different reasons than the benefits that the men will receive. Women have needs for certain nutrients at various stages of their lives, and eating a diet of clean foods will give them these nutrients. Before menopause, women need more iron to provide them with the energy they need to get through the day since iron will give them the healthy red blood cells that they need. During this time, a woman should eat lentils, beans, spinach, kale, fish, pork, turkey, chicken, and red meat. Women who are in the childbearing years need to load up on folic acid to help prevent congenital disabilities in the developing fetus. This will mean the woman will need to concentrate on eating whole-grain breads, brown rice, peas, beans, leafy greens, and citrus fruits. And a woman of any age will benefit from foods that are rich in vitamin D and calcium to keep their teeth and bones strong and healthy. Foods that are rich in vitamin D are plant-based milks, eggs, and fatty fish like salmon. Good sources of calcium include tofu, sardines, cheese, and yogurt as long as those foods come from clean sources. And, as women age, their requirements for calcium and vitamin D will increase.

Athletes and Body Builders

When athletes and body builders need more energy or are planning to set a goal for a new personal achievement, they need to make nutrition a top priority in their lives. A clean eating diet is a simple and sensible approach to allowing them to fulfill all of their goals. While it can take more preparation and planning for the athlete or the body builder, the clean eating diet will give them the good nutrition that they need to achieve their goals.

Whether an athlete is looking to maintain or lose weight, their goal should be to load up on healthy fats and lean proteins to fuel their energy needs without weighing them down like carbs will. The athlete will need to focus their attention on fatty fish, nuts, avocados, and lean protein like chicken. Athletes who are looking for more fuel for endurance will need to add in more good carbs. They will need to consume more high fiber foods like quinoa and brown rice and the low-carb veggies like cauliflower, broccoli, and leafy greens.

Body builders have specific protein needs because the muscles they are trying to increase are made of protein. Look to consume one and one half to two grams of protein for every pound that you currently weigh, and this formula works for both men and women who are body builders. This protein needs to come from as many sources as possible to ensure that a full range of nutrients is consumed along with the needed protein. Plan to pair a serving of chicken or fish with fiber-filled carbs like sweet potatoes, parsnips, turnips, or taro.

All Body Types

All body types will benefit from switching to a lifestyle of clean eating. The benefits go much further than simple weight control, although this is one of the perks of the clean eating meal plan. And it should be thought of as a meal plan, a lifestyle, and not a diet that you will stay on until you achieve whatever goal you are working on and then go back to your former diet of processed foods. Clean eating is a lifestyle of giving your body the nutrients that it needs to be happy, fit, and healthy. The clean eating lifestyle will give you numerous benefits.

A clean eating lifestyle will make you happier and more balanced. You need a healthy body to house your healthy mind. If you have ever been put into a bad mood just because you are tired, or sluggish, or in pain, then you will understand that statement fully. When you provide your body with all of the fuel that it needs to function properly, then your body will feel good, and your mind will feel good. Eating clean will also help to reduce your mood swings by helping your body reduce the release of cortisol, the stress hormone. This will make you feel healthier, fitter, and more balanced, and give you the energy to live your life to the fullest.

A clean eating lifestyle will give you a marvelous boost of energy. Think about the last time you ate something unhealthy and how your energy plummeted afterward. We have all suffered from the crash that comes from eating unhealthy processed or sugary foods, the simple carbs that cause the mid-afternoon energy crash. When you eat these foods for breakfast and lunch, they will immediately turn to sugar in your body and create a surge of energy as that blood sugar starts coursing through your body. When the body over-produces insulin to clear the sugar out of your blood, then you experience the crash that comes when the sugar is depleted. This leaves you not only feeling exhausted but craving more sugary treats. This puts you into a continuous cycle of always needing more and more sugar. When your meals are balanced and clean, you eliminate the spikes in blood sugar and the energy crashes that follow.

A clean eating lifestyle will free your taste buds. People who have busy lifestyles will often grab packaged and processed foods that they can eat while on the go. The problem with this is that these foods are created with the perfect amount of salt and sugar specifically designed to leave you craving more and more of the same foods. Our taste buds become addicted to these foods, and we become accustomed to those levels of fats, salts, and sugars. This can also cause you to look at healthy eating as being bland and tasteless. When you start eating clean and stick with it, then you will readjust your taste buds to accept the taste of real foods, and eventually, foods that you loved before will suddenly taste too sweet or too salty. You will soon enjoy the taste of real food, and you will not feel like you are missing anything.

A clean eating lifestyle will help prevent you from developing serious diseases. You will have a healthy body tomorrow if you start eating a clean diet today. Eating clean will benefit your body in so many ways. It will, perhaps most importantly, help to decrease the risk that you will develop some type of cardiovascular disease. These diseases, which include strokes, heart attacks, and high blood pressure, are some of the biggest killers today. People who eat an unhealthy diet face the risk of developing some type of cardiovascular disease, as well as certain cancers, arthritis, and diabetes. When you eat clean, you are making an investment in the quality of your life right now and the quality of your life in the future. You need to take care of your body since it is the one you will spend your entire life in.

A clean eating lifestyle will make you more productive. When your body is resting, your brain is still working, since it is in charge of running all of the functions that occur in your body. Your brain uses a lot of the energy that you take in. When the fuel you consume is good and clean your entire body will function better, and this includes your brain function. Unhealthy foods will cause a loss in the productivity levels in your brain. Good clean eating will boost the levels of productivity in your brain.

So start today on your new clean eating lifestyle so that you can take advantage of all of the benefits that clean eating has to offer. You need to care for your body since it is the place where you will live your life. Get started now on your new lifestyle so that you can reap all of the benefits it has to offer.

Chapter 3: Top Ten Tips For Eating Clean

Clean eating is a lifestyle choice that puts the focus on the whole, fresh foods. As long as you follow a few general guidelines, then you will enjoy this lifestyle and find it relatively easy to adhere to. You need to become accustomed to choosing real food, whole food, and minimally processed foods that will fill you full of the nutrients that your body needs. The plan is to eat foods that are at or close to their natural state. Here are ten easy-to-use tips that will get you started on the right path and make it relatively easy for you to make the switch to the clean eating lifestyle.

Water will now be your primary beverage. The most natural and the healthiest beverage that you can drink is water. It is naturally clean beverages that will keep you well hydrated and help you to lose weight effortlessly. Plain water has no questionable ingredients, no artificial sweeteners, sugars, or other additives. In contrast, beverages that are sweetened with sugar are consistently linked to high blood pressure, obesity, diabetes, and many other chronic illnesses. And due to its high content of sugar, juice may cause the same problems as other sugary beverages. When you follow a clean eating lifestyle, water should be the beverage that you drink the most.

Avoid foods in packages like snack foods. Pre-packaged, processed foods provide excess calories and very little nutritional value. If you follow a clean eating diet, then you will have no need for these foods in your diet. This will include snack cakes, cookies, muffins, granola bars, crackers, and any other food that is full of vegetable oils, sugar, salt, refined grains, and any other unhealthy substance that you can think of. You will need to practice always having healthy snacks available to prevent you from reaching for one of these unhealthy snacks when you are hungry between meals. Some good options for these healthy snacks are fruits, veggies, seeds, and nuts. These are all healthy options that taste good and will help you to fight off disease.

Eat more fruits and vegetables. Whenever possible, replace the refined grains in your recipes with veggies and have fruit for desserts and snacks. You can make noodles out of a zucchini or a sweet potato. Spaghetti squash is so named because it looks like spaghetti when it is cooked, so it makes a natural replacement for pasta. Cauliflower can be chopped into fine bits so that it can be used to create a crust for pizza, mashed like a white potato, or serves as a side dish instead of white rice.

Limit your consumption of alcohol. Certain types of alcohol, like wine, might be beneficial to your health if they are taken in small quantities. But, for the most part, frequently consuming alcoholic beverages can be damaging to your health. It can promote inflammation and lead you to several chronic diseases like excess belly fat, digestive disorders, and liver disease. Alcohol is the product of veggies, fruits, or grains that have been mixed with yeast and allowed to ferment, so alcohol is definitely not part of a clean eating lifestyle.

Stop adding extra sugar to your foods. If you really want to eat clean, then you will need to stop adding extra sugar to your foods. If your overall health allows it, then you can sometimes eat small amounts of maple syrup or honey, which are both natural sugar. If you have metabolic syndrome, diabetes, or any other health issues, then you may need to completely avoid any added sugar in your diet. Even natural sources of sugar do not contribute very much nutritional value. This will require label reading because you will find added sugar in most condiments and sauces. If you are really determined to follow a clean eating lifestyle, then you will learn to love the natural sweetness of fruit and to enjoy other foods and their unique flavors.

Leave the unhealthy fats out of your diet. Clean eating does not include consuming margarine and most vegetable oils since they are highly processed since they are produced through a process of chemical extraction. Also, some oils that are available commercially are loaded with linoleic acid, which is one of the omega-6 fatty acids. The omega-6 fatty acids are known to increase the levels of inflammation in your body, which can lead to an increased risk that you will develop heart disease or weight gain. You will need to consume some healthy fats on the clean eating lifestyle. You will want to concentrate on using olive oil and eating avocadoes, nuts, and fatty fish.

Eliminate the refined carbs from your diet. It is extremely easy to overeat when you are eating refined carbs. Unfortunately, they are highly processed foods that will give you very little in the way of nutrition. Obesity, fatty liver, insulin resistance, and inflammation have all been linked to the excess consumption of refined carbs. You will receive many more nutrients from whole grains as well as getting the good fiber that will improve the overall health of your gut and will help to reduce chronic inflammation. When you eat grains, you will need to choose the kinds that are the least processed such as steel-cut oats and sprouted grain bread.

Always read the nutritional labels on the foods that you buy. This is particularly important for two reasons. One, the food label will list the ingredients in the food and you will be able to see what salt, sugar, and chemicals have been added to that food. The second reason is that ingredients in foods may change over time, and something might be added in that you don't want to be eating. You will be buying some packaged foods like meats, nuts, seeds, and fruits and veggies, even though the bulk of your diet will be based on fresh foods. You will see that many nuts have been roasted in vegetable oils, which might mean that they have been damaged by the heat and the chemicals they were exposed to during processing. It is better to eat the nuts raw or roast them yourself in the oven at home. Pre-made salad mixes can be a real time-saver, but they may be covered in chemicals, and the dressing that is often included is certain to be full of salt and sugar.

Limit the amount of processed foods that you eat. The exact opposite of the clean eating lifestyle is the one where you consume processed foods, since processed foods are modified from their original, natural state. During processing, they gain salt, sugar, and other chemicals and lose many of their nutrients and fiber. Consuming processed foods can lead to an increased risk of developing heart disease and chronic inflammation. When you live a clean eating lifestyle, you will avoid processed foods as much as you possibly can.

Get used to eating real food. This is the basis of the clean eating lifestyle. You will eat food that is as close as possible to its natural state, so you will eat the apple and not the applesauce, or eat the orange instead of drinking the juice. Commercially produced juices are full of sugar and chemicals, so if you want to drink juice, make it at home. On the clean eating lifestyle you will enjoy whole, healthy foods that are free of preservatives, chemicals, salts, and sugars, and anything else that might be added to your food.

Eating a clean diet puts a heavy emphasis on minimally processed foods and nutritious fresh foods. You will learn to appreciate the natural flavor of the foods that you eat while your health enjoys the boost it will receive from the minerals and vitamins that you are consuming. Clean eating will offer you the best of all of the food groups without the additives you don't want or need.

Chapter 4: Clean Eating Myths to Avoid

Clean eating is a term that can be interpreted to mean things that it does not represent, or it might be open to misinterpretations. Some of these mistakes sound totally reasonable, like the idea that you can never eat 'bad' food again. To begin with, the food itself is not necessarily bad. Many people eat whatever they want to eat and live long, healthy lives. Some people need to analyze every bite they consume. There is no terrible food, just food you should avoid if you are following a clean eating lifestyle. But this does not mean you can never ever eat a cupcake again. Just do things in moderation. But there are definitely a few myths floating around that are completely incorrect and should be addressed.

Eating clean food does not always mean that you are eating healthy foods. You can make any food clean by using the proper ingredients, but that does not mean that the food is healthy for you. Desserts can contain fresh ingredients, but they are still desserts, and they are still full of sugar. When you are eating a clean diet, you will want to focus on foods that are good for your body, like whole grains, lentils and beans, olive oil and avocadoes, seeds and nuts, and fresh veggies and fruits. Even a clean sweet treat should be reserved for an occasional treat.

If you want to eat clean, then you must not eat gluten or dairy. There is absolutely no reason for you to avoid dairy products or foods that contain gluten unless you either don't like the taste or you have a medical reason to avoid them. Dairy and gluten do not make foods unhealthy. You can make a cake with no dairy or gluten, but that does not mean the cake is healthy; it is still a cake. So eat dairy products and gluten products if you want to.

You don't need to worry about molasses, maple syrup, and honey because they are not real sugar. There is something like fifty-six different names for the sugar that is added to your food, and molasses, maple syrup, and honey are just three of them. These are all different forms of sugar that use different names, but they are still sugar. They are not as highly processed as table sugar is, but when they arrive at your stomach, they are treated just the same as refined sugar, and they are digested quickly into blood glucose. You will need to limit your use of these just like you will eliminate any other sweetener.

Calories still count in the clean eating lifestyle. Some people think that as long as you are following a clean eating lifestyle, you do not need to worry about counting calories. But clean food is still full of calories. When you compare foods, you will find that some foods are more nutritious than other foods, so one hundred calories of soda are less nutritious than one hundred calories of flaxseeds, but they are both still one hundred calories. Just because your diet is nutritious does not mean the calories do not count. You will probably find it easier to lose weight on a clean eating lifestyle because you will be consuming more foods that are full of fiber and good carbs, which will keep you satisfied longer than sugary processed foods will. But it is still possible to follow a clean eating lifestyle and gain weight at the same time.

If your food is not organic, then it is full of GMOs.
A genetically modified organism (GMO) is any organism that has had its genetic makeup chemically altered to produce a different result. Plants are often changed so that they will grow faster or produce more abundant harvests. This is part of the reason that so many people push for organic foods, but just because a portion of food that you choose is not organic does not mean that it will be a GMO food. Some foods will have a higher chance of being GMO just because of their particular growing season or, in the case of some animals, the feed that they are fed. You can always buy organic foods or look for the verified seal that certifies that a particular food is non-GMO, but never be afraid to eat conventional foods.

Making a choice to follow the clean eating lifestyle is one that will take some adjustment and preparation but it will open the door to so many more options for good food than you may have ever seen before. Adopting a clean, eating way of life takes some planning to execute correctly, but it is not difficult. And when you make the choice to switch, then your body and your mind will be happier and healthier than ever before.

Chapter 5: Recipes For Breakfast

Anti-Inflammatory Spinach Cherry Smoothie

Prep five min/serves one

Vegetarian

Ingredients:

Chia seeds, one teaspoon plus one teaspoon
Ginger, ground, one tablespoon
Almond butter, unsalted, one tablespoon
Avocado, mashed, one fourth cup
Baby spinach leaves, one half cup
Cherries, frozen, one cup
Kefir, low-fat, one cup

Instructions:

Put the kefir in a blender and add in the ginger, almond butter, avocado, spinach, cherries, and one tablespoon of the chia seeds. Puree these ingredients until they make a smoothie that is creamy and smooth. Pour it into a glass for serving and garnish it with the other teaspoon of chia seeds.

Nutrition: Calories 410, 20 grams fat, 47 grams carbs, 17 grams protein

Tropical Mango Smoothie Bowl

Prep ten min/serves one

Vegetarian and vegan

Ingredients:

Coconut water, one third cup
Banana, frozen, one half of one
Pineapple, frozen, one half cup
Mango, frozen, one half cup
Coconut flakes, unsweetened, one tablespoon
Pomegranate seeds, two tablespoons
Pineapple, fresh and chopped, one fourth cup

Instructions:

Place into a blender the coconut water, frozen banana, frozen pineapple, and the frozen mango and puree all of these ingredients together until they are creamy and smooth. Pour the pureed smoothie into a bowl for serving and garnish it with the coconut flakes, pomegranate seeds, and the fresh chopped pineapple.

Nutrition: Calories 240, 4 grams fat, 4 grams protein, 54 grams carbs, 8 grams fiber

Tofu Scramble with Curry

Prep ten minutes/cook twenty minutes/serves four

Keto, low-carb, vegetarian

Ingredients:

SAUCE
Garam masala, one fourth teaspoon
Turmeric, ground, one fourth teaspoon
Paprika, ground, one fourth teaspoon
Coriander, ground, one fourth teaspoon
Cumin, ground, one fourth teaspoon
Garlic powder, one fourth teaspoon
Curry powder, one fourth teaspoon

SCRAMBLE
Spinach, roughly chopped, three cups
Onion, diced, one half medium
Olive oil, one tablespoon
Tofu, firm, eight-ounce block
Mushrooms, sliced, six ounces
Red bell pepper, diced and cleaned, one large

Instructions:

Press and drain the block of tofu for thirty minutes before beginning the recipe to remove all of the excess liquid in the block. Fry the onion in the olive oil for five minutes, and then add in the red peppers and the mushrooms and cook for an additional ten minutes. Push the cooked vegetables to one half of the skillet and put the tofu in the other half, breaking it into little chunks. Cook the tofu for five minutes. While the tofu is cooking, put all of the seasoning ingredients into a bowl and whip them together. Sprinkle this mixture over the ingredients in the skillet and mix all together. Add in the greens and cook this for five more minutes, and then serve.

Nutrition: Calories 118, 8 grams carbs, 11 grams protein, 4 grams fat

Spinach Mushroom Omelet

Prep three min/cook fifteen min/serves one to two

Keto, low-carb, vegetarian

Ingredients:

Olive oil, one tablespoon + one tablespoon
Red onion, diced, one quarter cup
Spinach, fresh, chopped, one and one half cup
Green onion, one diced
Mushrooms, button, five sliced
Eggs, three
Feta cheese, one fourth cup

Instructions:

Fry the onions, mushrooms, and spinach for three minutes in one tablespoon of olive oil and set to the side. Beat the eggs well and cook them in the other tablespoon of olive oil for three to four minutes until edges begin to brown. Sprinkle all the other ingredients onto half of the omelet and fold the other half over the sautéed ingredients. Cook for one minute on each side.

Nutrition info: Calories 337, 25 grams fat, 6 grams carbs, 22 grams protein

Cinnamon Roll Muffins

Prep five min/cook fifteen min/makes twenty muffins

Keto, low-carb, vegetarian, vegan

Ingredients:

MUFFINS
Almond flour, one half cup
Baking powder, one teaspoon
Cinnamon, one tablespoon
Coconut oil, one half cup
Nut butter or seed butter, one-half cup your choice: almond, sunflower, etc.

Pumpkin puree or unsweetened applesauce, one half cup
Vanilla protein powder, two scoops

GLAZE
Coconut butter, one-quarter of one cup
Lemon juice, two teaspoons
Milk, non-dairy of choice, one-quarter of one cup

Instructions:

Heat the oven to 350. Put paper cups into a twelve cup muffin pan and set it off to the side. Pour all of the listed dry ingredients into a large-sized mixing bowl and blend them well together. Then add in the list of wet ingredients and mix everything together well until the batter is smooth. Pour the batter carefully into the paper muffin cups, dividing the batter evenly among the twelve cups. Bake the muffins in the oven for ten to fifteen minutes. Leave the muffins in the pan to cool for the first five minutes, and then put them out onto a wired rack so they can finish cooling. As soon as the muffins are cool to the touch, then mix the ingredients for the glaze. Pour lines of the glaze over the cooled muffins and allow it to get hard, and then serve. These muffins need to be eaten within two days. If you would like to freeze them for later use just wrap each muffin individually.

Nutrition info per one muffin: Calories 112, 3 grams carbs, 5 grams protein, 9 grams fat

Low Carb Pancakes

Prep ten min/cook ten min/serves one

Keto, low-carb, vegetarian, vegan

Ingredients:

Almond butter, unsweetened, two tablespoons
Almond milk, unsweetened, one-fourth of one cup
Baking powder, one half teaspoon
Coconut flour, one tablespoon
Coconut oil, two tablespoons
Flax, ground, one tablespoon

Instructions:

Over a medium-high heat, set a large frying pan and add in the olive oil. Cream together the almond butter and the almond milk. In another bowl, mix together all of the dry ingredients until they are well mixed. Mix the milk and butter mixture into the dry ingredients, stirring well until all of the dry ingredients are wet. Let this mixture sit and rest for five minutes so that the coconut flour and the flax can absorb the excess liquid in the mix. Spoon the mix into the hot oil to fry the pancakes; the batter should make three or four pancakes. Fry the pancakes for four to five minutes on each side. You will want to see small bubbles all over the top in the batter before you flip it over. Top the pancakes with the topping of your choice like fresh fruit, vegan butter, or sugar-free syrup.

Nutrition info per recipe: Calories 260, 21 grams fat, 10 grams protein, 5 grams carbs

Hearty Breakfast Salad

Prep thirty min/serves four

Vegetarian

Ingredients:

Eggs, four hard-boiled
Lemon, one
Prep thirty min/serves four

Ingredients:

Eggs, four hard-boiled
Lemon, one
Arugula, ten cups
Quinoa, one cup cooked and cooled
Olive oil, two tablespoons
Dill, chopped, one half cup
Almonds, chopped, one cup
Avocado, one large sliced thin
Cucumber, chopped, one half cup
Tomato, one large cut in wedges

Instructions:

Mix together the quinoa, cucumber, tomatoes, and arugula. Toss these ingredients lightly along with the olive oil, and pepper. Divide the salad between four plates for serving and arrange the egg and avocado on top. Top each salad with almonds and herbs. Drizzle with juice from the lemon.

Nutrition info: Calories 336, 8 grams fat, 55 grams carbs, 12 grams protein

Poached Salmon Egg Toast

Prep ten min/cook four min/serves two

Low-carb

Ingredients:

Bread, two slices rye or whole-grain toasted
Lemon juice, one quarter teaspoon
Avocado, two tablespoons mashed
Black pepper, one quarter teaspoon
Eggs, two poached
Salmon, smoked, four ounces
Scallions, one tablespoon sliced thin

Instructions:

Add the lemon juice to the avocado and stir in the pepper. Spread the avocado mixture over the toasted slices of bread. Lay the smoked salmon over the toast and top each slice with a poached egg. Top everything with the sliced scallions.

Nutrition info: Calories 389, 17 grams fat, 32 grams carbs, 34 grams protein

Egg Muffins with Feta and Quinoa

Prep fifteen min/cook thirty min/serves six to twelve

Keto, low-carb, vegetarian

Ingredients:

Eggs, eight
Baby spinach, chopped, two cups
Tomatoes, chopped, one cup
Onion, chopped, one quarter cup
Black olives, chopped, one quarter cup
Feta cheese, one cup
Quinoa, one cup cooked
Olive oil, two teaspoons
Oregano, fresh chop, one tablespoon

Instructions:

Heat the oven to 350. Spray oil a muffin pan with twelve cups. Cook the olives, onion, spinach, oregano, and tomatoes for five minutes in the olive oil over medium heat. Beat the eggs. Add the cooked mix of veggies to the eggs with the cheese. Spoon the mix evenly into the muffin cups. Bake the muffins for thirty minutes. These will remain edible and fresh in the fridge for two days. To eat the next day, just wrap the muffin in a paper towel and warm it in the microwave for thirty seconds.

Nutrition info one muffin: Calorie 113, 5 grams carbs, 6 grams protein, 7 grams fat

Honey Almond Ricotta with Peaches

Prep fifteen min/serves four to six

Vegetarian and vegan

Ingredients:

SPREAD
Ricotta, skim milk, one cup
Almonds, thin slices, one half cup
Almond extract, one quarter teaspoon
Honey, one teaspoon

TO SERVE
Peaches, sliced, one cup
Bread, whole grain bagel or toast

Instructions:

Mix the almond extract, honey, ricotta, and the almonds. Spread one tablespoon of this mix on the slice of toasted bread and cover it with the peaches.

Nutrition info: Calories 230, 8 grams fat, 37 grams carbs, 9 grams protein

Cauliflower Hash Browns

Prep five min/cook ten min/serves six

Vegetarian and vegan

Ingredients:

Cauliflower, one half of one head broken into small pieces
Chickpea flour, one-quarter of one cup
Coconut oil, one tablespoon
Cornstarch, one tablespoon
Garlic powder, one half teaspoon
Onion, one half chopped

Instructions:

Heat the oven to 400. Lay aluminum foil or parchment paper on a cookie sheet. Lightly spray the covering with spray oil. Grate the cauliflower and the onion until they are finely grated. Put this mixture into a large-sized bowl. Combine in the garlic powder, cornstarch, and chickpea flour and mix until the ingredients are well blended. Separate the batter into six equal-sized portions and form them into patty shapes. Set the patties on the cookie sheet and bake for twenty minutes. Turn them over and bake for twenty more minutes.

Nutrition info per patty: Calories 144, 6 grams fat, 6 grams protein, 20 grams carbs

Maple Oatmeal

Prep five min/cook twenty min/serves four

Keto, low-carb, vegetarian, vegan

Ingredients:

Almond milk, one-third of one cup
Walnuts, one half of one cup
Chia seeds, four tablespoons
Sunflower seeds, unsalted, three tablespoons
Cinnamon, one teaspoon
Pecans, one half of one cup
Coconut flakes, unsweetened, one-quarter of one cup
Maple flavoring, one teaspoon

Instructions:

Crumble the pecans, walnuts, and sunflower seeds in a food processor. Set a large-sized sauce pot on the stove and place the nuts into it after they have pulsed. Blend in well the remainder of the ingredients and then turn the heat on under the pot to medium. Simmer the mixture for thirty minutes while you stir often. This is needed so that the chia seeds will not stick to the bottom. Serve the hot oatmeal with a sprinkle of cinnamon if so desired.

Nutrition info per serving: Calories 374, 4 grams carbs, 10 grams protein, 35 grams fat

Mediterranean Style Breakfast Burrito

Prep fifteen min/ cook five min/serves six

Low-carb, vegetarian, vegan

Ingredients:
Avocado oil, two tablespoons
Tortillas, ten-inch size, low carb, six
Black olives, sliced, three tablespoons
Tomatoes, chopped, three tablespoons
Nutritional yeast, one half of one cup
Spinach, two cups, washed and dried
Refried beans, canned, three-fourths of one cup
Salsa for garnish

Instructions:

Fry the spinach, black olives, and tomatoes in a large skillet in the avocado oil for five minutes while you are stirring constantly. Put two tablespoons of the refried beans on each of the tortillas and spread it over the tortillas, going just to one inch from the edge. Divide the veggie mix evenly over the tortillas. Roll each one up by folding the sides in and then rolling the tortilla. Put them back in the skillet with the leftover olive oil and fry the rolled burritos for three minutes on each side. Serve them with the salsa if desired.

Nutrition info per burrito: Calories 252, 19 grams carbs, 14 grams protein, 11 grams fat

Baked Eggs with Tomato and Spinach

Prep five minutes/cook twenty minutes/serves two

Keto, low-carb, vegetarian

Ingredients:
Eggs, two

Black pepper, one-half teaspoon
Red pepper flakes, one teaspoon
Basil, fresh, chop, one-half cup
Balsamic vinegar, two tablespoons
Olive oil, one tablespoon
Cheddar cheese, one-half cup
Onion, small, one
Tomatoes, four medium
Spinach, two cups

Instructions:

Heat the oven to 400. Chop the tomatoes and dice the onions and mix them together, then stir in the spinach. Stir in everything else except for the eggs and stir everything together well. Spoon this mix into two pans that are oven safe and make a small indent in the middle. Crack the eggs, adding one to each pan. Bake for twenty minutes.

Nutrition: Calories 237, 14 grams protein, 10 grams carbs, 14 grams fat

Poached Egg with Avocado

Prep two min/cook ten min/serves one

Keto, low-carb, vegetarian

Ingredients:
Black pepper, one fourth teaspoon
Egg, one
Avocado, one half mashed

Instructions:

Mash the avocado half and spoon it onto a plate. Poach the egg and lay it on top of the mashed avocado.

Nutrition: Calories 407, 15 grams protein, 7 grams carbs, 23 grams fat

Spinach Mozzarella Frittata

Prep fifteen min/cook twenty min/serves four to six

Keto, low-carb, vegetarian

Ingredients:

Mozzarella cheese, shredded, one cup
Onion, diced, one half cup
Spinach, one cup diced
Almond milk, one half cup
Eggs, eight
Olive oil, two tablespoons

Instructions:

Heat the oven to 450. Fry the spinach and the onions in the olive oil for five minutes. While they are frying, beat the eggs and milk in a bowl. Place the spinach onion mix into a greased nine by nine-inch baking dish. Pour the eggs over the spinach mix and cover the eggs with the shredded cheese. Bake the frittata for twenty minutes.

Nutrition: Calories 315, 7 grams carbs, 22 grams protein, 22 grams fat

Italian Skillet Eggs

Prep five min/cook ten min/serves two

Vegetarian and low-carb

Ingredients:
Parmesan cheese, grated, one fourth cup
Olive oil, one tablespoon
Mozzarella cheese, six ounces shredded
Garlic, minced, two tablespoons
Eggs, four
Black pepper, one half teaspoon
Red pepper flakes, one fourth teaspoon
Diced tomatoes, one twenty-eight ounce can

Instructions:

Fry the garlic and red pepper flakes in the olive oil for two minutes. Pour in the can of tomatoes with the juice and stir in the pepper. Simmer until the mix begins to bubble, then cook it for five more minutes. Make four holes with the back of a spoon and crack one egg into each of the wells. Sprinkle both kinds of cheese over the mix and cook for ten minutes.

Nutrition: Calories 620, 15 grams carbs, 42 grams protein, 35 grams fat

Huevos Rancheros

Prep fifteen min/cook fifteen min/serves four

Low-carb and vegetarian

Ingredients:

Olive oil, one tablespoon + one tablespoon
Cilantro, fresh chopped, one fourth cup
Onion, chopped, one fourth cup
Feta cheese, crumbled, one fourth cup
Eggs, four
Garlic powder, one tablespoon
Tomatoes, one large diced
Jalapeno pepper, one diced
Oregano, dried, one teaspoon
Tomato paste, one tablespoon
Cumin, ground, one teaspoon

Instructions:

Fry the garlic and the onions in one tablespoon of olive oil for five minutes, stirring frequently. Add in the oregano, jalapeno, tomato paste, and cumin and mix well for one minute. Pour in the diced tomatoes and simmer for four more minutes. In another skillet heat the other tablespoon of olive oil and fry the eggs for five minutes turning only once. Place spoons of the warm sauce on a plate and top with one fried egg, then sprinkle the eggs with the cilantro and the feta cheese.

Nutrition: Calories 198, 15 grams carbs, 12 grams protein, 9 grams fat

Scrambled Tofu with Peppers and Onions

Prep five min/cook five min/serves two

Low-carb, vegetarian, vegan

Ingredients:

Olive oil, one tablespoon
Red bell pepper, one diced
Cilantro, fresh, one third cup
Black pepper, one teaspoon
Tofu, extra firm, eight ounces
Onion, diced, one half cup
Cheddar cheese, shredded, one-half cup or nutritional yeast, one half cup

Instructions:

Fry the chopped peppers and onions in the olive oil for five minutes over medium heat. While they are frying, squeeze the excess liquid out of the tofu and break it up into small chunks. Add the pieces of tofu to the onions and peppers in the skillet and scramble until they are warmed through, about six minutes, stirring often. Stir the cheese or nutritional yeast with the cilantro into the tofu mixture, mix well and serve.

Nutrition: Calories 369. 14 grams carbs, 20 grams protein, 26 grams fat

Buckwheat Berry Pancakes

Prep fifteen min/cook ten min/serves three to four

Low-carb, vegetarian, vegan

Ingredients:

Coconut oil, two tablespoons
Banana, one
Buckwheat flour, two cups
Milk, coconut or almond, one and one half cups
Vanilla extract, one teaspoon
Baking powder, one teaspoon
Turmeric, ground, three teaspoons
Cardamom, ground, one half teaspoon
Blueberries, fresh or thawed frozen, unsweetened, one cup

Instructions:

Mash the banana until smooth. Stir in the milk and vanilla. In a separate large bowl, mix the buckwheat flour, baking powder, cardamom, and turmeric just until blended. Add in the wet ingredients and stir gently until the two are just mixed. Warm the oil in a large skillet over medium heat and add in the batter, using two tablespoons for each pancake. Cook each pancake for three to four minutes or until the top is mostly covered with bubbles and then flip to cook on the other side. Serve the pancakes with the blueberries on top.

Nutrition per four cakes: Calories 150, 4 grams fat, 12 grams carbs, 4 grams protein

Quiche Cups

Prep ten min/cook thirty min/makes twelve cups
Keto, low-carb, vegetarian, vegan

Ingredients:

Cornstarch, one tablespoon
Tomato paste, one tablespoon
Water, three tablespoons
Dijon mustard, two tablespoons
Tofu, extra firm, one block (fourteen ounces)
Garlic powder, two teaspoons
Spinach, frozen, thawed, four cups
Lemon juice, one tablespoon
Nutritional yeast, one half of one cup

Instructions:

Heat the oven to 350. Put paper cups in all of the cups of a twelve cup muffin pan and set it to the side. Toss together all of the listed ingredients into a blender except for the spinach and blend them on high until the mixture is creamy and smooth. Put the spinach into a large bowl and then pour the mix from the blender into the bowl. Stir the liquid mix together with the spinach and then divide this mix into the twelve muffin cup papers, making them as even as possible. Bake the muffins for thirty to thirty-five minutes or until just the edges are turning slightly brown.

Nutrition info per muffin: Calories 57, 2 grams fat, 3 grams carbs, 6 grams protein

Sweet Potato Hash Egg Muffin

Prep ten min/cook fifteen min/serves eight

Keto, low-carb, vegetarian

Ingredients:

Black pepper, one half teaspoon
Sweet potato, one small, grated
Eggs, eight
Cheddar cheese, one fourth cup
Garlic powder, one half tablespoons
Spray oil

Instructions:

Heat the oven to 375. Use spray oil to grease the cups of an eight cup muffin pan or use paper cups. Grate the sweet potato. Mix in a bowl the cheddar cheese, garlic powder, and sweet potato. Scoop out one tablespoon of this mix for each of eight cups in the muffin pan. Then break one egg into each cup. Bake these muffins for twelve to sixteen minutes or until the egg is cooked the way you prefer.

Nutrition: Calories 103, 8 grams protein, 4 grams carbs, 6 grams fat

Vegetable Quiche

Prep twenty-five min/cook one hour/serves six

Keto, low-carb, vegetarian

Ingredients:

Parmesan cheese, grated, two tablespoons
Olive oil, two tablespoons
Cheddar cheese, three-fourths cup
Onion, diced fine, one half cup
Black pepper, one teaspoon
Almond milk, one half cup

Squash, peeled and sliced, one cup (one large)
Eggs, four
Thyme, ground, one tablespoon
Garlic, minced, two tablespoons
Orange bell pepper, one, cleaned and diced
Zucchini, peeled and sliced, one cup (one large)

Instructions:

Heat the oven to 350. Fry the minced garlic, bell pepper, thyme, onion, squash, and zucchini for five minutes while you are stirring often. While this is frying beat the black pepper and the milk with the egg until they are well mixed. Pour the fried veggies into a greased nine by nine baking dish and top with the cheddar cheese. Cover this with the egg mix and then the parmesan cheese. Bake for fifty minutes and then let the quiche cool for ten minutes before you cut it.

Nutrition: Calories 240, 12 grams protein, 11 grams carbs, 9 grams fat

Tomato Omelet

Prep two min/cook eight min/serves one

Keto, low-carb, vegetarian

Ingredients:

Eggs, two
Olive oil, two tablespoons
Basil, fresh, one half cup
Cherry tomatoes, one half cup
Cheese, any type, one-quarter cup shredded
Black pepper, one teaspoon

Instructions:

Cut the tomatoes into quarters. Fry the tomatoes in the olive oil for three minutes and then set the tomatoes off to the side. In a small bowl, add the pepper to the eggs and beat together well. Pour the beaten egg mixture into the pan and use a spatula to gently work around the edges under the omelet, letting the eggs fry unmoved for three minutes. When just the center third of the egg mix is still runny, add on the basil, tomatoes, and cheese. Fold over half of the omelet onto the other half. Cook two more minutes and serve.

Nutrition: Calories 342, 8 grams carbs, 20 grams protein, 25 grams fat

Kiwi Strawberry Smoothie

Prep ten min/serves one

Vegetarian and vegan

Ingredients:

Kiwi, peeled and chopped, one
Strawberries, fresh or frozen, one-half cup chopped
Milk, almond or coconut, one cup
Basil, ground, one teaspoon
Turmeric, ground, one teaspoon
Banana, diced, one
Chia seed powder, one quarter cup

Instructions:

Drink the smoothie immediately after pureeing all of the ingredients in your blender on high until smooth.

Nutrition: Calories 250, 1 gram fat, 34 grams carbs, 3 grams protein

Carrot Cake Overnight Oats

Prep five min/set overnight/serves one

Vegetarian

Ingredients:

Coconut or almond milk, one cup
Cinnamon, ground, one teaspoon
Vanilla extract, one teaspoon
Chia seeds, one tablespoon
Carrot, one large peel, and shred
Raisins, one half cup

Cream cheese, low fat, two tablespoons at room temperature
Steel-cut oats, one half cup

Instructions:

Mix together all of the listed ingredients and store the oats in a refrigerator safe container overnight. Eat cold in the morning. If you choose to warm this, just microwave for one minute and stir well before eating.

Nutrition: Calories 340, 4 grams fat, 70 grams carbs, 8 grams protein

Quinoa Breakfast Bowl

Prep thirty minutes/serves six

Vegetarian

Ingredients:

Quinoa, two cups cooked
Olive oil, one teaspoon
Black pepper, one teaspoon
Eggs, twelve
Greek yogurt, plain, one quarter cup
Garlic, minced, one teaspoon
Baby spinach, chopped, one cup
Feta cheese, one cup
Cherry tomatoes, one pint cut in halves

Instructions:
Mix together the garlic, onion powder, eggs, pepper, and yogurt. Cook the spinach and tomatoes for five minutes in the olive oil over medium heat. Pour in the

egg mix and stir until eggs have set to your preferred doneness. Mix in quinoa and feta until they are hot. This will store in the fridge two to three days.

Nutrition: Calories 340, 7 grams fat, 59 grams carbs, 11 grams protein

Kale Tofu Scramble

Prep five min/cook ten min/serves one

Keto, low-carb, vegetarian, vegan

Ingredients:

Olive oil, two tablespoons
Kale, shredded, one half cup
Tofu, extra firm, four ounces
Sprouts, one half cup
Garlic, minced, one tablespoon
Black pepper, one quarter teaspoon
Turmeric, ground, one tablespoon

Instructions:

Press the liquid from the tofu and break it into pebble-sized pieces, and add in the black pepper, turmeric, and garlic. Fry the kale in the olive oil over medium heat for five minutes, and then stir the mixture with the tofu into the skillet with the kale. Continue cooking, stirring often, until the tofu is well mixed and warm. Top with the raw sprouts and serve.

Nutrition: Calories 137, 8 grams fat, 8 grams carbs, 13 grams protein

Ginger, Carrot, and Turmeric Smoothie

Prep five min/serves two

Vegetarian and vegan

Ingredients:

Cayenne pepper, one eighth teaspoon
Orange, one, peeled and separated
Turmeric, ground, one teaspoon
Carrot, one large, peeled and chopped
Ginger, ground, one teaspoon
Mango, fresh or frozen chunks, one half cup
Hemp seeds, raw, shelled, one tablespoon
Coconut water, one cup

Instructions:

Puree all of the ingredients together with one-half cup of ice until smooth and drink immediately.

Nutrition per one cup: Calories 250, 5 grams fat, 48 grams carbs, 6 grams protein

Pear Spiced Oatmeal

Prep fifteen min/serves one

Low-carb, vegetarian, vegan

Ingredients:
Cinnamon, one teaspoon
Pear, fresh, sliced, one fourth cup
Ginger, ground, one eighth teaspoon

Steel-cut oats, one-fourth cup before preparing, prepared

Instructions:

Place the cooked oats into a bowl and stir in the ginger until it is well mixed. Top the cooked oatmeal with the pears and then sprinkle the cinnamon over the pears and the oatmeal.

Nutrition: Calories 108, 2 grams fat, 21 grams carbs, 3 grams protein

Bonus Recipe -- Homemade Bagels

Prep ten min/cook forty min/makes six

Keto, low-carb, vegetarian, vegan

Ingredients:

Baking powder, one teaspoon
Ground flaxseed, one half of one cup
Psyllium husks, one-quarter of one cup
Tahini, one half of one cup
Water, one cup

Instructions:

Heat the oven to 375. Cover a cookie sheet by wrapping it with aluminum foil or laying parchment paper over it. Blend well together in a medium-sized mixing bowl, the baking powder, salt, ground flax seeds, and the psyllium husks and stir together until they are combined well. In another smaller bowl cream together the tahini and the water. Pour the mixed-together wet ingredients into the mixed- together dry ingredients in the larger bowl and mix them well until they form the dough. Divide the ball of dough into six lumps of dough that are all about the same size. With your hands gently flatten all of the lumps until they are rounded into patties and about one-quarter inch thick. Lay each of the patties on the cookie sheet and use a small circular item to cut a small round shape out of the middle of each one. Bake the bagels for forty to forty-five minutes or until they turn a golden brown. Let the bagels cool before you eat them, and top them any way you would like to or eat them plain.

Nutrition info per bagel: Calories 209, 16 grams fat, 2 grams carbs, 7 grams protein

Chapter 6: Recipes For Lunch

These are all quick and easy recipes for lunch so that you will not be tempted to keep working and miss this meal!

Herbed Cheese and Tomato Salad

Prep ten min/serves four

Keto, low-carb, vegetarian, vegan

Ingredients:

Basil ground, one teaspoon
Black pepper, one teaspoon
Tomatoes, eight large sliced in half
Paprika, ground, one teaspoon
Olive oil, two tablespoons
Parsley, two tablespoons, chopped
Mozzarella cheese, sliced eight slices
Lemon, one half

Instructions:

Season the sliced halves of the tomatoes by drizzling on the lemon juice and then sprinkling on the black pepper and the basil. Lay two tomato halves on each serving plate with the inside facing up. Lay one cheese slices on top of each tomato half and then garnish them with the parsley and paprika, then dribble the olive oil over everything.

Nutrition: Calories 196, 15 grams fat, 8 grams carbs, 9 grams protein

Chicken Salad Stuffed Peppers

Prep thirty min/ serves six

Low-carb

Ingredients:

Bell peppers, three of any color, halved and seeded
Celery, four stalks sliced thin
Parsley, fresh, chopped, one third cup
Cucumber, one half diced
Rice vinegar, two tablespoons
Dijon mustard, two tablespoons
Cherry tomatoes, one pint cut in quarters
Greek yogurt, low fat, two-thirds cup
Scallions, one bunch sliced thin
Chicken breast, cooked, two cups cubed
Black pepper, one half teaspoon

Instructions:

Blend together in one bowl the rice vinegar, mustard, yogurt, black pepper, and parsley and let this sit for thirty minutes for the flavors to blend together. Then mix into this the scallions, cucumbers, tomatoes, celery, and chicken. Spoon this chicken mixture into the bell pepper halves.

Nutrition: Calories 116, 3 grams fat, 16 grams carbs, 7 grams protein

Chicken Kebabs

Prep fifteen min/cook fifteen min/serves four

Keto, low-carb; exchange the chunks of chicken with tofu or tempeh to make it vegetarian and vegan

Ingredients:

Black pepper, one teaspoon
Marjoram, one-half teaspoon
Tomatoes, grape or cherry, one pound
Olive oil, four tablespoons
Mushrooms, button, one pound whole
Rosemary, one teaspoon
Onions, white pearl, one pound
Turmeric, one teaspoon
Chicken breast, boneless and skinless, two pounds cut
into chunks

Instructions:

Mix together in a small bowl, the pepper, turmeric, marjoram, and rosemary. Place the tomatoes, mushrooms, onions, and chunks of chicken onto wooden or metal skewers, alternating the ingredients in any way that you like. Brush all sides of the food with the olive oil using a pastry brush and then sprinkle on the mixture of seasonings. Cook the skewers for fifteen minutes under the broiler, on an outdoor grill, or in a grill pan on the stovetop, turning often to prevent burning.

Nutrition per skewer: Calories 240, 23 grams protein, 7 grams carbs, 11 grams fat

Grilled Eggplant Rolls

Prep five min/cook eight min/serves eight

Keto, low-carb, vegetarian, vegan

Ingredients:

Basil, dried, two tablespoons
Tomato, one large
Black pepper, one teaspoon
Olive oil, two tablespoons
Thyme, one-half teaspoon
Eggplant, one medium-sized

Instructions:

Peel the eggplant and cut off both ends so that the ends are flat. Slice the eggplant from one end to the other end in slices that are about one-eighth of an inch thick. Slice the tomato into eight thin slices, sprinkle the thyme on the tomato slices, and then set them off to the side. Carefully brush the olive oil on the slices of the eggplant using a pastry brush. Fry the slices of eggplant in a hot skillet for three minutes on each side. When all of the slices have been fried on both sides lay a slice of tomato on each of the slices of eggplant. Sprinkle the black pepper and the basil over the tomato slices and the eggplant and then roll up the slices of eggplant with the tomatoes inside.

Nutrition per one roll: Calories 59, four grams carbs, 3 grams protein, 3 grams fat

Lime Cilantro Slaw Salad

Prep ten min/serves five

Keto, low-carb, vegetarian, vegan

Ingredients:

Avocados, two
Cilantro leaves, fresh, chopped finely, one cup
Green cabbage, one-half head shredded
Purple cabbage, one-half head shredded
Garlic, minced, two tablespoons
Rosemary, one teaspoon
Paprika, one teaspoon
Lime juice, two tablespoons
Water, one-quarter of one cup

Instructions:

Mix the chopped cilantro leaves with the minced garlic. Peel the avocados after wiping them off and remove the pits and throw the pits away. Mash the pulp of the avocados and cream the pulp together with the water and the lime juice. Stir in the minced garlic and cilantro to make a dressing that is smooth and creamy. Add in the green cabbage and the purple cabbage and toss it with the dressing mix gently but completely. Put the coleslaw salad in the refrigerator for at least one hour before serving it.

Nutrition: Calories 119, 3 grams protein, 3 grams carbs, 9 grams fat

Zucchini Noodles with Avocado Sauce

Prep ten min/serves two

Low-carb, vegetarian, vegan

Ingredients:

Avocado, one
Water, one-third of one cup
Basil, freshly chopped, one and one fourth cup
Cherry tomatoes, twelve sliced in thirds
Pine nuts, four tablespoons
Lemon juice, two tablespoons
Zucchini, one or one pound of frozen zucchini noodles thawed and dried

Instructions:

If you are using a fresh zucchini, the wipe off the skin of the zucchini and then peel it. Then either uses a vegetable peeler or a spiralizer cutter to cut the zucchini into spiral noodles that look like spaghetti. Wipe off and peel the avocado, throwing away the pit.

Mix the water, lemon juice, pine nuts, basil, and the avocado pulp into a blender. Puree all of these ingredients together until they make a smooth sauce. Put the zucchini noodles into a large bowl and pour the creamy sauce from the blender over them. Mix the noodles together well but gently. When they are fully mixed, toss in the cherry tomato slices and then serve this immediately. You can also save this salad for serving later, but don't keep it for more than two days.

Nutrition: Calories 313, 19 grams carbs, 26 grams fat, 7 grams protein

Veggie and Cheese Toast

Prep five min/serves one

Vegetarian and vegan

Ingredients:

Balsamic vinegar, one teaspoon
Avocado, one mashed
Oregano, dried, one fourth teaspoon
Cucumber, one half diced
Cumin, one fourth teaspoon
Rosemary, one fourth teaspoon
Tomato, one half diced
Whole grain flatbread, two slices
Black pepper, one half teaspoon
Olive oil, one teaspoon

Instructions:

Blend the olive oil, black pepper, rosemary, cumin, and the oregano into the mashed avocado. Spread this mixture on the two slices of flatbread after you toast them. Lay the diced tomato and the diced cucumber on top of the spread avocado. Drizzle on vinegar to taste.

Nutrition: Calories 177, 24 grams carbs, 8 grams fat, 3 grams protein

Pepper and Onion Pasta

Prep ten min/cook ten min/serves four

Low-carb, vegetarian, vegan

Ingredients:

Whole wheat pasta, any shape, twelve ounces
Parsley, dried, one tablespoon
Whole peeled tomatoes, one fourteen ounce can with juice
Red bell pepper, one chopped
Yellow bell peppers, two chopped
Crushed red pepper, one fourth teaspoon
Black pepper, one fourth teaspoon
Cumin, one teaspoon
Olive oil, three tablespoon
Garlic, minced, one tablespoon
Onion, sweet yellow, diced, one half cup

Instructions

Cook the pasta per the package directions. Fry the onion, garlic, and crushed red pepper, in the hot olive oil in a large skillet for ten minutes. Stir in the tomatoes, black pepper, cumin, and peppers and cook all of this for fifteen minutes. Mix in the parsley and stir for one minute, and then take the skillet off the heat. Toss this mixture with the pasta and serve.

Nutrition: Calories 135, 3 grams fat, 4 grams protein, 22 grams carbs

Chicken Cutlets with Mashed Yams

Prep fifteen min/cook fifteen min/serves four

General diet

Ingredients:

Chicken cutlets, one pound
Olive oil, two tablespoons
Yams, two large
Almond milk, one half cup
Broccoli, three cups steamed

Black pepper, one teaspoon
Turmeric, one tablespoon
Vegetable broth, one cup
Lemon juice, two tablespoons
Garlic, minced, one tablespoon
Rosemary, one teaspoon
Almond flour, one quarter cup

Instructions:

Stab a few holes in the yams with a fork and microwave them for ten minutes on high. While the yams are cooking mix together the seasonings. Use this mixture to season the cutlets and then coat them with flour. Fry the cutlets in the olive oil over medium heat for ten minutes on each side. When the yams are soft, scoop out the flesh into a small bowl and mix well with the milk. Lay the cutlets on a serving plate and put the chicken on a paper towel to drain. Add the minced garlic to the skillet for thirty seconds. Add the broth and lemon juice to the skillet and cook for three minutes. Spoon this sauce over the chicken and serve.

Nutrition: Calories 300, 36 grams fat, 2 grams carbs, 30 grams protein

Baked Fish with Veggies

Prep five min/cook twelve min/serves two

Keto and low-carb

Ingredients:

FISH INGREDIENTS
Whitefish fillets, two six-ounce skinless boneless

Olive oil, two tablespoons
Red onion, three slices
Capers, drained, two teaspoons
Black olives, one half cup
Artichokes, one cup

DRY RUB

Black pepper, one quarter teaspoon
Cinnamon, one quarter teaspoon
Sage, ground, one quarter teaspoon
Nutmeg, one quarter teaspoon
Onion powder, one quarter teaspoon
Garlic powder, one teaspoon
Thyme, dried, one teaspoon

Instructions:

Heat the oven to 425. Mix together the dry rub ingredients, mixing them well in a small bowl. Tear off two sheets of aluminum foil just over one foot wide (about fourteen inches). Lay one fish fillet on each foil sheet. Sprinkle each fillet with one tablespoon of the dry rub. Place the olives, artichokes, onions, and capers over the fish fillets, and then sprinkle them with the remainder of the dry rub. Dribble the olive oil over the veggies. Wrap the foil packets closed by pulling all four sides to the top of the fish and rolling the pouch closed. Bake the pouches for fifteen minutes on a cookie sheet.

Nutrition: Calories 180, 10 grams carbs, 63 grams fat, 23 grams protein.

Sloppy Joes

Prep ten min/cook fifteen min/serves four

Keto and low-carb

Ingredients:

Ground beef, one pound
Whole grain or rye bread or rolls
Tomato paste, one fourth cup
Worcestershire sauce, two teaspoons
Vegetable broth, low-sodium, three quarters cup
Celery, one stalk diced finely
Garlic, minced, two tablespoons
Black pepper, one teaspoon
Cumin, one teaspoon
Thyme, one half teaspoon
Yellow onion, one small diced finely

Instructions:

Break the meat into small bits as you stir it around, cooking the ground beef until it is browned completely, for about ten minutes. When the meat is thoroughly cooked, stir in the onion, celery, and garlic and cook this mixture for five more minutes. Blend in the remainder of the list of ingredients and mix them together well. Turn the heat down to low and let the mix simmer for twenty minutes until it begins to thicken. Serve the sloppy joes on rye or whole grain bread or rolls.

Nutrition: Calories 240, 5 grams net carbs, 8 grams fat, 36 grams protein.

Hamburger Brussel Sprouts Gratin

Prep ten min/cook twenty min/serves four

Keto and low-carb

Ingredients:

Ground beef, one pound
Parsley, one tablespoon
Brussel sprouts, fifteen ounces, cut in half
Cumin, one teaspoon
Cheddar cheese, shredded, one cup
Italian seasoning, one tablespoon
Thyme, one half teaspoon
Greek yogurt, low fat, four tablespoons
Black pepper, one teaspoon
Olive oil, two tablespoons

Instructions:

Heat the oven to 425. Fry the Brussel sprouts in the heated olive oil over medium heat for five minutes. Stir in the Greek yogurt and mix this together well and then pour this mixture into an olive oil spritzed eight by eight-inch baking pan. Cook the ground beef thoroughly and season it with the pepper, then add this mix to the mix in the baking pan. Top with the shredded cheese and sprinkle on the herbs. Bake the casserole for twenty minutes.

Nutrition: Calories 770, 8 grams net carbs, 62 grams fat, 42 grams protein.

Cauliflower Fried Rice

Prep five min/cook ten min/serves four

Keto, low-carb, vegetarian, vegan

Ingredients:

Tofu, firm, pressed and chopped into small pieces, four ounces
Carrot, one-quarter of one cup chopped fine
Garlic, minced, two tablespoons
Red bell pepper, one cleaned and diced finely
Green onion, one-quarter of one cup
Sesame oil, toasted, one teaspoon
Soy sauce, low-salt, two tablespoons
Olive oil, two tablespoons
Riced cauliflower, twelve ounces frozen or fresh
Black olive, diced, one fourth cup

Instructions:

Into a large skillet over a medium-high heat, place the olive oil with the chopped carrots and the riced cauliflower. Cook these together for five minutes, stirring them often. Into this mix, you will add the minced garlic and the chopped green onions and stir them in well. Cook all of this mix for another three minutes. Now stir in the small pieces of tofu and mix them in well with the other ingredients. Cook the mix with the tofu for five minutes, just to warm the tofu. Pour in the sesame oil and the soy sauce, stir these in quickly, and then serve sprinkled with the black olives.

Nutrition info per serving: Calories 114, 6 grams carbs, 4 grams protein, 8 grams fat.

Squash and Sweet Potato Patties

Prep fifteen min/cook ten min/serves two

Keto, low-carb, vegetarian, vegan

Ingredients:

Applesauce, unsweetened, one half cup
Sweet potato, shredded, one cup
Avocado oil, two tablespoons
Squash, shredded, one cup
Black pepper, one teaspoon
Cumin, ground, one quarter teaspoon
Rosemary, dried, one half teaspoon
Garlic powder, one half teaspoon
Parsley, dried, one quarter teaspoon

Instructions:

Blend together well the sweet potato, squash, and applesauce together in a large mixing bowl. Stir in the garlic powder, cumin, parsley, rosemary, and pepper and mix these seasonings in thoroughly. Set a large-sized skillet on the stove over a medium-high heat and pour in the olive oil. While it is warming, divide the mixture in the bowl into four portions of equal size. When the olive oil is hot, set each portion in the skillet in the hot oil and press the portions down gently until they are one half to one inch thick. Let the portions fry for five minutes before gently turning them over. Fry them on the other side for five minutes and serve them while they are hot.

Nutrition info per patty: Calories 112, 6 grams carbs, 3 grams protein, 9 grams fat

Nicoise Salad

Prep twenty min/serves four

Low-carb and vegetarian

Ingredients:

SALAD
Hard-boiled eggs, two sliced
Black pepper, one half teaspoon
French-style green beans, four ounces
Red onion, thin-sliced, one half cup
Black olives, pitted, one fourth cup
Basil, dried, two tablespoons
Olive oil, one tablespoon
Bibb lettuce, one large head
Grape tomatoes, one cup
Red potato wedges, twelve ounces

DRESSING
Lemon juice, two tablespoons
Water, one tablespoon
Olive oil, three tablespoons
Garlic, minced, one tablespoon
Rosemary, one teaspoon
Cumin, one teaspoon

Instructions:

Use a small bowl to mix all of the ingredients for the dressing and then refrigerate. Cook the green beans for two minutes in water and then drain them well.

Using a large skillet over a medium heat warm the olive oil and cook the potatoes for five minutes each side, stirring them well and often. Arrange the Bibb lettuce leaves evenly on four plates and sprinkle them with the dried basil. Divide the green beans, olives, potatoes, onions, eggs, and tomatoes evenly over the four plates. Sprinkle the black pepper over each salad and then serve with the chilled dressing.

Nutrition: Calories 413, 10 grams fat, 21 grams carbs, 19 grams protein

Vegetarian Nachos

Prep fifteen minutes/serves six

Low-carb, vegetarian, vegan

Ingredients:

Oregano, fresh, one tablespoon minced

Red onion, two tablespoons minced
Black olives, two tablespoons chopped
Feta cheese or nutritional yeast, one-fourth cup crumble
Grape tomatoes, one-half cup cut into quarters
Romaine lettuce, one cup chopped
Pita chips, three cups whole grain
Black pepper, one fourth teaspoon
Lemon juice, one tablespoon
Olive oil, two tablespoons
Hummus, one-third cup prepared

Instructions:

Blend together the lemon juice, olive oil, black pepper, and hummus in a bowl. Spread the pita chips out on a platter. Use a spoon to drizzle three-fourths of the hummus mixture over the pita chips. Garnish the chips with the feta cheese or the nutritional yeast, tomatoes, red onion, olives, and lettuce. Spoon the remainder of the hummus decoratively in the middle of the pita chips and garnish everything with the oregano.

Nutrition info one serving: Calories 159, 10 grams fat, 13 grams carbs, 4 grams proteins

Mediterranean Pasta

Prep five min/cook fifteen min/serves four to six

Vegetarian and vegan

Ingredients:

Parsley, fresh chopped, one fourth cup
Parmesan cheese or nutritional yeast, one fourth cup

Lemon juice, one fourth cup
Red pepper flakes, one half teaspoon
Black pepper, one half teaspoon
Olive oil, three tablespoons
Black olives, six ounces whole pitted
Artichoke hearts, one fourteen ounce can quartered
Grape tomatoes, two cups
Garlic, minced, three tablespoons
Rosemary, one teaspoon
Nutmeg, one teaspoon
Angel hair pasta, whole wheat, six ounces cooked

Instructions:

Save half of the water that the pasta was cooked in. During the time the pasta is cooking, get the veggies ready by slicing the cherry tomatoes in half, chopping the artichokes, and slicing the olives. Use a large skillet to cook the black pepper, garlic, red pepper flakes, and tomatoes for three to five minutes. Drop the drained pasta into the skillet and stir everything together rapidly. Mix in the olives, lemon juice, and artichokes. If this pasta mix seems to be a bit dry, then use some of the saved pasta water to loosen it. When all of the ingredients are well mixed together, take the skillet from the heat and garnish with the parsley and the Parmesan cheese or the nutritional yeast.

Nutrition: Calories 267, 13 grams fat, 27 grams carbs, 18 grams protein.

Chicken Quinoa Bowl

Prep thirty min/serves four

General diet

Ingredients:

Parsley, finely chop, two tablespoons
Black pepper, one half teaspoon
Chicken breast, one pound cooked, boneless and skinless
Feta cheese, one-fourth cup crumbled
Cucumber, diced, one cup
Almonds, slivered, one fourth cup
Roasted red peppers, one seven-ounce jar rinsed
Red onion, fine chopped, one fourth cup
Black olives, pitted and chopped, one fourth cup
Garlic, minced, one tablespoon
Olive oil, four tablespoons divided
Quinoa, two cups cooked
Red pepper, crushed, one fourth teaspoon
Cumin, ground, one fourth teaspoon
Paprika, one teaspoon

Nutrition:

Place the chicken breast on a plate and shred it or slice it very thin. While the chicken is broiling puree, the cumin, almonds, paprika, garlic, red pepper, and roasted peppers with two of the tablespoons of olive oil until it is creamy and smooth. Use a bowl to mix the olives, quinoa, red onion, and the other two tablespoons of the olive oil very well. Spoon the mixture with the quinoa into four bowls, making them evenly divided. Top the quinoa with the chicken and the cucumber. Drizzle on the red pepper sauce. Garnish with parsley and feta.

Nutrition: Calories 519, 27 grams fat, 31 grams carbs, 34 grams proteins

Philly Cheese Steak

Prep ten min/cook ten min/serves four

Keto and low-carb

Ingredients:

Olive oil, one tablespoon
Sirloin steak, one pound
Black pepper, one teaspoon
Yellow onion, one small sliced paper-thin
Provolone cheese, low fat, four slices
Green pepper, one medium cleaned and sliced thinly
Whole grain bread, four slices, or four sub rolls

Slice the steak into very thin strips, about one-eighth of an inch thick and season the strips with the pepper. Fry the steak strips in the olive oil over medium heat and cook them until they are browned, between five and ten minutes. Take the steak from the skillet and place it on paper towels to drain, and add in the green peppers and the onion and fry these for five minutes. Put one slice of cheese on each slice of whole-grain bread or sub roll and top the cheese with the steak slices and the onion and green pepper mixture.

Nutrition: Calories 350, 18 grams fat, 3 grams net carbs, 42 grams protein

Chickpea and Cranberry Salad

Prep twenty min/serves four

Keto, low-carb, vegetarian, vegan

Ingredients:

Black pepper, one teaspoon
Cucumber, chopped, one cup
Red onion, sliced thin, one half of one cup
Cherry tomatoes, red, one cup cut in halves
Parsley, fresh, chopped, one-quarter of one cup
Cherry tomatoes, yellow, one cup cut in halves
Olive oil, two tablespoons
Chickpeas, one cup drained and rinsed
Lemon juice, two tablespoons
Cranberries, one cup washed and sliced in halves

Instructions:

Toss the chickpeas, cucumber, onion, cranberries, and tomatoes in a medium-sized mixing bowl. In a separate smaller bowl, stir together well the parsley, lemon juice, olive oil, and pepper. Pour the bowl of wet ingredients over the bowl of dry ingredients and toss to mix them together gently but very well.

Nutrition: Calories 145, 9 grams carbs, 4 grams protein, 8 grams fat.

Thai Soup

Prep ten min/cook fifteen min/serves four

Keto low-carb, vegetarian, vegan

Ingredients:

Bell pepper, red, one-half cut in julienne strips
Cilantro, one half of one cup chopped
Coconut milk, one fourteen ounce can
Garlic, minced, two tablespoons
Ginger, ground, one tablespoon
Lime juice, two tablespoons
Mushrooms, three sliced thinly
Onion, red, one-half cut in julienne strips
Tamari, one tablespoon
Thai chili, finely chopped, one half of one
Tofu, firm, pressed and cubed, ten ounces
Vegetables broth, two cups

Instructions:

Set a Dutch oven or a large cooking pot on the stove and turn on the heat to medium-high. Pour in the coconut milk and the vegetable broth and mix them together well. Stir in the garlic, ground ginger, mushrooms, Thai chili, red bell pepper, and onion and mix all of these ingredients together well. Right when the liquid begins to boil, keep stirring often and let the soup cook for five minutes. Now add in the tofu and let the mix cook for another five minutes. Take the pot of soup off of the heat and stir in well the lime juice, cilantro, and the tamari. Mix these in well and then serve the soup.

Nutrition: Calories 339, 15 grams protein, 8 grams carbs, 27 grams fat

Salmon with Quinoa and Vegetables

Prep ten min/cook twenty min/serves four

Low-carb

Ingredients:

SALMON
Parsley, fresh chop, one fourth cup
Black pepper, one fourth teaspoon
Lemon, one cut into eight wedges
Cumin, one teaspoon
Salmon fillets, four fillets of five ounces each
Paprika, one half teaspoon

QUINOA
Quinoa, one cup cooked per package directions
Lemon zest, two tablespoons
Cucumbers, three-fourths cup diced
Basil, dried, two teaspoons
Red onion, one-fourth cup diced fine
Cherry tomatoes, one cup sliced in half

Instructions:

Heat the oven to 400. Use olive oil spray oil on a nine by thirteen inch baking dish. Put the fish fillets in the baking dish. Mix the cumin, pepper, and paprika in a small bowl and sprinkle on the fish. Lay the lemon wedges around the fish. Spoon the cooked quinoa around the fish. Use a medium bowl to toss together the basil, onions, lemon zest, tomatoes, and cucumber and pour this mixture over the fish and the quinoa. Bake this dish for twenty minutes.

Nutrition: Calories 222, 4 grams fat, 16 grams carbs, 32 grams protein

Spinach Macaroni Cheese

Prep five min/cook twenty min/serves four

Vegetarian and vegan

Ingredients:

Parsley, chopped for garnish
Black pepper, one half teaspoon
Italian seasoning, one half teaspoon
Almond milk, one cup
Vegetable broth, one cup
Elbow macaroni, whole wheat, two cups
Feta cheese or nutritional yeast, one cup
Baby spinach, fresh, eight to ten ounces
Tomatoes, two fresh, diced
Garlic, minced, two tablespoons
Onion, one small finely diced
Olive oil, two tablespoons

Instructions:

Cook the garlic and onions in hot olive oil for five minutes. Stir in seasonings, milk, broth, macaroni, cheeses, spinach, and tomatoes. Boil this mix while you are stirring frequently, then turn down the heat and simmer this mixture for fifteen minutes. Stir often, about every two to three minutes, or the mixture will stick to the pan. Sprinkle the macaroni mixture with parsley and serve.

Nutrition: Calories 544, 23 grams fat, 60 grams carbs, 22 grams protein

Black Bean and Sweet Potato Rice Bowl

Prep thirty min/serves four

Vegetarian and vegan

Ingredients:

Sweet chili sauce, two tablespoons
Black beans, one fifteen ounce can drain and rinse
Kale, fresh, four cups chopped
Red onion, one fine chop
Olive oil, three tablespoons
Water, one and one half cups
Garlic powder, one half teaspoon
Long grain rice, three-fourths cup uncooked

Instructions:

Cook the rice in water with the garlic powder for twenty minutes. While the rice cooks put the sweet potato in the hot olive oil in a skillet and cook for eight minutes, stirring often. Mix in the onion, kale, and beans and cook five more minutes. Stir in the sweet chili sauce into the cooked rice and add this to the potato mix and serve.

Nutrition info for two cups cooked: Calories 453, 11 grams fat, 10 grams protein, 74 grams carbs.

Korean Steak

Prep five min/cook ten min/serves four

Keto and low-carb

Ingredients:

Cumin, ground, one tablespoon
Sesame oil, three tablespoons
Sirloin steak, one pound sliced thinly
Ginger, ground, one tablespoon
Sesame seeds, two tablespoons
Scallions, two thin sliced

Instructions:

Season the steak pieces with the ginger and the cumin. Heal the sesame oil in a large skillet over a medium heat. Mix in the scallions and stir repeatedly for two minutes. Then blend in the steak pieces and stir often while cooking the steak for eight minutes. Serve with a tossed salad or some mixed veggies.

Nutrition: Calories 350, 3 grams fat, 30 grams protein, 4 grams carbs

Cherry Apple Pork Medallions

Prep thirty min/cook twenty min/serves four

General diet

Ingredients:

Apple cider vinegar, one tablespoon
Pork tenderloin, one pound
Olive oil, one tablespoon
Brown rice, eight ounces cooked
Apple, one large sliced thin
Celery powder, one half teaspoon
Apple juice, unsweetened, two-thirds cup
Thyme, dried, one quarter teaspoon
Cherries, dried tart, one half cup
Rosemary, dried, one quarter teaspoon

Instruction:

Slice the tenderloin into twelve slices of equal size and sprinkle them with rosemary, celery powder, and thyme. Cook the slices of pork in hot olive oil for three minutes each side; remove them from the skillet and set them to the side. Add in the vinegar, apple juice, cherries, and apple slices in the skillet and mix everything together well. Boil the mix, then turn down the heat and simmer for five minutes. Put the pork back into the skillet and cook for five more minutes. Serve the pork mixture with the cooked rice.

Nutrition info for three ounces cooked pork and one-third cup of rice: Calories 349, 9 grams fat, 37 grams carbs, 25 grams protein

Ham Cheese and Chive Soufflé

Prep ten min/cook thirty min/serves four

Keto and low-carb

Ingredients:

Olive oil spray oil
Ham, fully cooked, diced, two cups
Chives, chopped fresh, two tablespoons
Cheddar cheese, low fat, shredded, one cup
Eggs, six large
Black pepper, one teaspoon
Greek yogurt, one half cup
Garlic, minced, two tablespoons
Yellow onion, one small peeled and diced
Olive oil, two tablespoons

Instructions:

Heat the oven to 400. Use olive oil spray to grease four six-ounce ramekins or other oven-safe dishes. Fry the onion and the garlic over medium heat in the olive oil for five minutes. Mix together the diced ham, chives, cheddar cheese, onion, and garlic in a bowl. Beat together the yogurt with the eggs and pour this over the ham mixture in the bowl. Then add the fried garlic and onion to the bowl and mix everything together very well. Divide the mixture among the oven dishes and cook them for thirty minutes.

Nutrition: Calories 460, 5 grams net carbs, 38 grams fat, 24 grams protein

Stuffed Artichokes

Prep forty min/cook thirty min/serves six

Low-carb and vegetarian

Ingredients:

Artichokes, three

Parsley, chopped, one tablespoon
Chili sauce, one tablespoon
Rosemary, ground, one teaspoon
Egg, one slightly beaten
Cottage cheese, low fat, one half cup
Onion, minced, two tablespoons
Celery powder, one quarter teaspoon
Mushroom, chopped, one half cup
Lemon juice, two tablespoons

Instructions:

Heat the oven to 375. Peel off and throw away the outside leaves of the artichokes. Cut the inside of the artichokes in half across the middle. Drop the artichoke halves into a pot of boiling water and cook them for twenty minutes. Mix together in a bowl the mushrooms, onions, cottage cheese, egg, lemon juice, chili sauce, parsley, and the seasonings and spoon this mixture into the boiled artichoke hearts. Place the filled hearts into a baking pan and bake them for thirty minutes.

Nutrition: Calories 425, 17 grams carbs, 18 grams protein, 21 grams fat

Stuffed Zucchini with Goat Cheese and Marinara

Prep ten min/cook ten min/serves four

Keto, low-carb, vegetarian

Ingredients:
Zucchini, medium-sized, four
Parsley, chopped, to garnish with
Black pepper, one half teaspoon
Rosemary, one teaspoon
Cumin, one teaspoon
Marinara sauce, one cup
Goat cheese, sixteen ounces

Instructions:

Heat the oven to 400. Cut the zucchinis down the length in half and scoop out the seeds. Sprinkle on the rosemary, pepper, and cumin. Place four ounces of the goat cheese in each zucchini and cover with one-fourth cup of the marinara sauce. Bake the zucchinis for ten minutes.

Nutrition: Calories 81, 3 grams protein, 6 grams carbs, 5 grams fat

Chickpea Salad

Prep twenty min/serves four

Keto, low-carb, vegetarian, vegan

Ingredients:

Chickpeas, one cup drained and rinsed
Cucumber, chopped, one cup
Cherry tomatoes, red, one cup cut in halves
Parsley, fresh, chopped, one quarter cup
Red onion, sliced thin, one half cup
Cherry tomatoes, yellow, one cup cut in halves
Olive oil, two tablespoons
Turmeric, ground, one teaspoon
Lemon juice, two tablespoons
Black pepper, one teaspoon

Instructions:

Mix the chickpeas, onion, cucumber, and tomato together in a medium-sized mixing bowl. Add in the parsley, turmeric, lemon juice, and black pepper to the veggies in the bowl and mix together well.

Nutrition: Calories 145, 9 grams carbs, 4 grams protein, 8 grams fat.

Chapter 7: Recipes For Dinner

Okra and Corn Casserole

Prep twenty min/cook thirty min/serves six

Low-carb, vegetarian, vegan

Ingredients:

Okra, one pound
Black pepper, one teaspoon
Cumin, ground, one teaspoon
Green bell pepper, one cleaned and sliced
Corn, whole kernel, one can
Onion, one small, sliced
Parsley, chopped, one tablespoon
Avocado, three tablespoons
Garlic, minced, one tablespoon
Tomatoes, two large diced

Instructions:

Heat the oven to 375. Cut the okra into bite-sized pieces. Cook the garlic, okra, onion, cumin, and green pepper in the avocado oil for ten minutes. Stir in the parsley and the tomatoes and cook for an additional ten minutes. Mix in the corn and pour the entire mixture into a nine by nine baking pan and bake, not covered, for thirty minutes.

Nutrition: Calories 125, 17 grams carbs, 4 grams protein, 2 grams fat.

Chicken with Balsamic Tomato Sauce

Prep thirty-five minutes/serves four

Keto and low-carb

Ingredients:

Chicken breast, two eight-ounce boneless skinless
Fennel seeds, toasted, one tablespoon
Whole wheat flour, one fourth cup
Garlic, minced, one tablespoon
Olive oil, three tablespoons divided
Broth, chicken, low sodium, one cup
Cherry tomatoes, one-half cup sliced in half
Black pepper, one half teaspoon
Rosemary, one half teaspoon
Balsamic vinegar, one fourth cup
Shallots, sliced, two tablespoons
Instructions:

Cut both chicken breasts in half the long way, then pound them with a meat mallet until each breast is about one-fourth inch thick. Sprinkle the chicken breasts with the pepper and the rosemary. Cover the breasts with the flour (throw away rest of the flour). Fry the chicken in two tablespoons of the hot olive oil in a large skillet for five minutes on each side until the chicken is brown. Lay chicken on a plate, cover it with aluminum foil to keep it warm, and set the chicken to the side. Put in the rest of the olive oil and put the tomatoes, shallot, and vinegar in the skillet and cook for one minute. Add the garlic, fennel seeds, and the broth. Cook this mixture for ten minutes, stirring in the butter as it cooks. Cover the chicken pieces with the sauce to serve.

Nutrition: Calories 294, 17 grams fat, 9 grams carbs, 25 grams proteins

Hasselback Caprese Chicken

Prep twenty five min/cook twenty-five min/serves four

Keto and low-carb

Ingredients:

Olive oil, two tablespoons
Chicken breast, two boneless and skinless
Broccoli florets, eight cups
Marjoram, one half teaspoon
Thyme, one half teaspoon
Pesto, prepared, one fourth cup
Black pepper, one-fourth teaspoon and one fourth teaspoon
Mozzarella, fresh, three ounces halved and sliced
Tomato, one medium sliced

Instructions:

Heat the oven to 375. Use spray oil to grease a cookie sheet. Cut evenly spaced slices across each chicken breast about one-half inch apart from one end to the other. Sprinkle the chicken breasts with the black pepper, thyme, and marjoram. Fill the cut places on the chicken alternating with the cheese and tomato. Coat each of the chicken breasts with the pesto. Lay the chicken down one side of the cookie sheet. Put the olive oil and the broccoli in a bowl and toss well until the broccoli is well coated. Put the broccoli on the empty side of the cookie sheet, adding in any tomatoes that are leftover. Bake the chicken and the broccoli for thirty minutes.

Nutrition: Calories 355, 19 grams fat, 10 grams carbs, 38 grams protein

Grape Tomatoes and Spiral Zucchini

Prep five min/cook ten min/serves two

Keto, low-carb, vegetarian, vegan

Ingredients:

Zucchini, one large cut in spirals
Tarragon, one teaspoon
Black pepper, one teaspoon

Grape tomatoes, one cup cut in half
Crushed red pepper flakes, one quarter teaspoon
Thyme, one half
Garlic, minced, two tablespoons
Olive oil, one tablespoon
Basil, fresh, chopped, one tablespoon

Instructions:

Fry the minced garlic in the olive oil for one minute. Add in the tarragon, black pepper, red pepper flakes, thyme, and the tomatoes and mix well and then lower the heat. Simmer this mix for fifteen minutes. Stir in the basil and the zucchini spiral noodles, and then turns the heat back up to high and cook the mixture for two minutes, stirring constantly.

Nutrition: Calories 117, 13 grams carbs, 4 grams protein, 5 grams fat

Roasted Root Veggies

Prep twenty min/cook thirty min/serves four to six

Vegetarian and vegan

Ingredients:

Sweet potato, one large, sliced thin
Black pepper, one teaspoon
Turnip, two medium-sized, peeled and chunked
Rosemary, ground, one teaspoon
Parsnips, three medium, peeled and sliced
Nutmeg, one teaspoon
Carrots, four medium, peeled and cut into chunks
Cinnamon, one teaspoon

Beets, red, peeled and cut into chunks
Olive oil, one tablespoon

Instructions:

Heat the oven to 425. Blend together in a large sized bowl all of the vegetables after they have been cut up. Drizzle the olive oil on the veggies and mix them around to coat all of the veggies. Add in the nutmeg, rosemary, and cinnamon and mix well again. Use spray oil to oil a thirteen by nine-inch baking dish and put the veggies into it. Bake the veggies for thirty minutes, stirring them every ten minutes. When the veggies have finished cooking, then sprinkle the black pepper on to them and put them in a large bowl to serve.

Nutrition: Calories 196, 4 grams fat, 3 grams protein, 40 grams carbs

Bean Bolognese

Prep fifteen min/cook twenty min/serves four

Vegetarian and vegan

Ingredients:

White beans, one fourteen ounce can drain and rinse
Parmesan cheese or nutritional yeast, grated, one half cup
Fettuccini, whole wheat, eight ounces
Parsley, fresh, chopped, one-quarter cup divided
Tomatoes, diced, one fourteen ounce can
Bay leaf, one
Garlic, four cloves peeled and chopped

Celery, one-quarter cup chopped fine
Carrot, one-half cup chopped fine
Onion, one small chopped fine
Olive oil, two tablespoons

Instructions:

Cook the pasta per the package directions. Cook the celery, onion, garlic, and carrot in the olive oil for ten minutes. Add in the bay leaf and stir the veggies for one minute. Remove the bay leaf and throw it away. Add the beans, tomatoes, and two tablespoons of the parsley to the skillet and mix them in well, and then simmer this mixture for five minutes, stirring often. Spoon the pasta into four serving bowls. Top the pasta with the sauce mix from the skillet. Top with the rest of the parsley and the parmesan.

Nutrition: Calories 442, 11 grams fat, 68 grams carbs, 18 grams protein

Grilled Pork Tenderloin

Prep ten min/cook twenty min/serves four to six

Keto and low-carb

Ingredients:

Pork tenderloin, two to three pounds
Olive oil, one quarter cup
Apple cider vinegar, one half cup
Black pepper, one teaspoon
Garlic, minced, two tablespoons
Dijon mustard, three tablespoons
Red pepper flakes, one teaspoon

Instructions:

In a large bowl to mix together the red pepper flakes, garlic, black pepper, mustard, apple cider vinegar, and olive oil until well blended. Place the pork tenderloin into this mixture and let it set in the refrigerator overnight. The next day takes the tenderloin out of the marinade and let it come to room temperature before grilling. Throw away the marinade. Grill the pork tenderloin for ten minutes on each side or until a meat thermometer reads 160 degrees in the tenderloin. Allow the tenderloin stand for ten minutes before slicing it. Serve the slices of pork tenderloin with the Dijon mustard.

Nutrition: Calories 340, 13 grams fat, 11 grams carbs, 43 grams protein

Butternut Squash with Mustard Vinaigrette

Prep twenty min/cook fifty min/serves six

Keto, low-carb, vegetarian, vegan

Ingredients:

Butternut squash, three small peeled, seeded and cut in half
Black pepper, one teaspoon
Cumin, one teaspoon
Shallots, eight, cut into wedges
Parsley, chopped, one quarter cup
Dry mustard, one tablespoon
Rosemary, one teaspoon
Balsamic vinegar, one tablespoon

Olive oil, four tablespoons

Instructions:

Heat the oven to 375. Mix the squash and the shallots in a large mixing bowl with the pepper, rosemary, cumin, and olive oil, tossing the veggies to mix them well and coat all of the pieces. Arrange the shallots and squash on a cookie sheet and bake them for fifty minutes. While the veggies are baking make a vinaigrette with the parsley, balsamic vinegar, and the dry mustard. Arrange the baked veggies on a serving dish and drizzle the vinaigrette over them and serve.

Nutrition: Calories 135, 1 gram protein, 11 grams carbs, 10 grams fat

Tex Mex Stuffed Zucchini Boats

Prep ten min/cook thirty min/serves four

Keto and low-carb

Ingredients:

Ground beef, one pound
Cilantro, fresh, chopped fine, one half cup
Shredded cheese, cheddar, one and one quarter cups
Zucchini, two
Tex Mex seasoning, two tablespoons
Olive oil two tablespoons

Instructions:

Heat the oven to 400. Wash and dry both zucchini and then cut each zucchini in half down the length and take out the seeds. Fry the ground beef in the olive oil over medium heat until it is well cooked, about ten minutes. Stir in the salt and the Tex Mex seasoning and let the meat cook until all of the liquid has cooked away. Use spray oil to oil a nine by thirteen inch baking pan and lay the zucchini halves in it with the cut side facing up. Stir one-third of the shredded cheese and the cilantro into the meat mix. Fill the halves of the zucchini evenly with the meat and cheese mix. Use the leftover of the shredded cheese to sprinkle on the top. Bake for twenty minutes.

Nutrition: Calories 601, 6 grams carbs, 49 grams fat, 33 grams protein

Spicy Lentil Soup

Prep twenty min/cook fifty min/serves eight

Low-carb, vegetarian, vegan

Ingredients:

Black pepper, one teaspoon
Celery, fine chop, one half of one cup
Vegetable broth, seven cups
Yellow onion, one chopped fine
Cilantro, chopped, one half of one cup
Parsley, fresh, chopped, one half of one cup
Tomato, two large, cleaned and diced
Cinnamon, one tablespoon
Ginger, two tablespoons minced
Olive oil, three tablespoons
Paprika, one tablespoon
Lentils, dry, one half of one cup

Instructions:

Set a large skillet over medium heat on the stove and add in the olive oil. Then fry the onion, garlic, ginger, and celery for ten minutes while you stir the mix frequently. Mix in the pepper, turmeric, paprika, and the cinnamon and cook the mix for five more minutes. Pour in the vegetable broth and add in the cilantro, tomatoes, and the lentils. Mix this all together well and let the soup simmer over a lowered heat for thirty minutes.

Nutrition info per two cups of soup: Calories 240, 15 grams carbs, 14 grams protein, 8 grams fat.

Zucchini Lasagna

Prep twenty min/cook one hour/serves nine

Keto, low-carb, vegetarian, vegan

Ingredients:

FOR THE RICOTTA
Tofu, extra firm, one sixteen ounce block drained and pressed for ten minutes
Basil, finely chopped fresh, one half of one cup
Oregano, dried, two teaspoons
Water, one half of one cup
Black pepper, one teaspoon
Lemon juice, two tablespoons
Olive oil, one tablespoon
Nutritional yeast, two tablespoons
OTHER INGREDIENTS

Zucchini, three medium sliced paper-thin from end to end
Marinara sauce, one twenty eight-ounce jar

Instructions:

Heat the oven to 375. Crumble the block of tofu and put it in a blender or large mixing bowl. Add the oregano, basil, lemon juice, olive oil, water, pepper, and the nutritional yeast to the tofu. Mix these ingredients together until the mixture looks like a creamy paste. Use olive oil spray oil to grease a nine by thirteen inch baking dish. Pour into the baking dish one cup of the marinara sauce and spread it around. Cover the marinara sauce with thin slices of the zucchini. Drop small amounts of the tofu ricotta mix over the zucchini and gently spread it around until the strips of zucchini are almost all covered. Pour some more of the marinara sauce over the tofu ricotta mix and then lay on another layer of the slices of zucchini. Keep making more layers until all of the slices of zucchini and all of the fillings have been used up. The two layers that are on the top should be marinara sauce on top of zucchini. Cover this dish with aluminum foil and put it in the oven. Bake the zucchini lasagna for forty-five minutes and then remove the foil covering and bake it for another fifteen minutes. Cut it into nine squares the moment you take it out of the oven and sprinkle the top with more of the chopped fresh parsley.

Nutrition info per square: Calories 338, 34 grams fat, 10 grams carbs, 5 grams protein

Tofu in Tomatoes

Prep five min/cook twenty min/serves two

Low-carb, vegetarian, vegan

Ingredients:

Thyme, one quarter teaspoon
Tomatoes, one fifteen ounce can diced
Black pepper, one teaspoon
Olive oil, one tablespoon
Rosemary, one teaspoon
Chili powder, one quarter teaspoon
Oregano, one teaspoon
Garlic, minced, two tablespoons
Tofu, one block medium, unpressed, cut into rounds one half-inch thick

Instructions:

Fry the minced garlic for two minutes in the hot olive oil. Blend in the rosemary, chili powder, thyme, oregano, pepper, and the tomatoes, mixing these ingredients together well. After they are well-mixed turn down the heat under the skillet so the mixture can simmer. Let it simmer for five minutes. Lay the rounded slices of tofu into the tomato mixture and then let the mix simmer undisturbed for fifteen minutes, or until the sauce is somewhat thick and the tofu has begun to get soft.

Nutrition: Calories 284, twenty grams protein, sixteen grams carbs, ten grams fat

Greek Style Spaghetti Squash

Prep forty min/cook thirty min/serves two

Low-carb, vegetarian, vegan

Ingredients:

Avocado oil, two tablespoons
Thyme, dried, one half teaspoon
Cherry tomatoes, eight, each cut in three slices
Spinach, fresh or frozen chopped finely, one cup
Chickpeas, one-third of one cup, drained and rinsed
Spaghetti squash, one large
Garlic, minced, one tablespoon
Nutritional yeast, two tablespoons
Rosemary, dried, one teaspoon
Onion, red, one-quarter of one cup sliced thinly
Marjoram, dried, one teaspoon

Instructions:

Heat the oven to 400. Wipe off the outside of the spaghetti squash and then cut it in half from one end to the other end. Scoop out the seeds with a spoon. Lightly oil the insides of the squash with one tablespoon of the avocado oil. Completely cover a baking sheet with parchment paper or aluminum foil. Lay the spaghetti squash on the cookie sheet with the inside facing down. Use a fork to poke three or four holes into the skin of the squash, and then bake the squash for thirty minutes. When the squash is done use the tines of a fork to scrape the cooked flesh out of the spaghetti squash; it will look like spaghetti. Put the stringed squash in a bowl and set it off to the side. Fry the onion and the garlic in the last tablespoon of the avocado oil for five minutes, stirring occasionally. Then blend in the rosemary, marjoram, thyme, tomatoes, and chickpeas and cook this mix for five more minutes. Mix in the spinach and the spaghetti squash and stir constantly while you cook this for five more minutes. Sprinkle the nutritional yeast on top and serve while the dish is hot.

Nutrition: Calories 272, 11 grams protein, 14 grams carbs, 10 grams fat

Creamy Curry Noodles

Prep ten min/cook ten min/serves four

Low-carb, vegetarian, vegan

Ingredients:

CREAMY CURRY SAUCE
Apple cider vinegar, two tablespoons
Avocado oil, two tablespoons
Black pepper, one half teaspoon
Coriander, ground, one and one half teaspoons
Cumin, ground, one teaspoon
Curry powder, two teaspoons
Ginger, ground, one quarter teaspoon
Tahini, one-quarter of one cup
Turmeric, ground, one teaspoon
Water, one-quarter of one cup

NOODLE BOWL
Bell pepper, red, one cleaned and diced
Carrots, two, peeled and cut in julienne strips
Cauliflower, one half of one head chopped small

Cilantro, fresh, chopped small, one half of one cup
Kale, two cups packed
Zucchini noodles, one sixteen ounce pack

Instructions:

Cover the zucchini noodles with two cups of boiling water in a large bowl. Set this bowl off to the side. After five minutes, drain off the water and then put the hot noodles back into the bowl. After prepping the veggies toss the bell pepper, carrots, cilantro, and cauliflower into the noodles. Lay the kale leaves onto four individual serving plates. Put together all of the ingredients for the Curry Sauce and mix it well in a mixing bowl. Pour the creamy sauce over the ingredients in the large mixing bowl with the noodles and toss everything together gently but very well. Divide the noodle mix over the kale leaves on the plates and serve.

Nutrition: Calories 192, 16 grams carbs, 15 grams fat, 5 grams protein

Portobello Mushroom Tacos

Prep twenty min/cook ten min/yields six tacos

Low-carb, vegetarian, vegan

Ingredients:

TACOS
Portobello mushrooms, one pound
Cumin, ground, one teaspoon
Onion powder, one teaspoon
Green collard leaves, six

Olive oil, three tablespoons divided
Harissa, mild or spicy, one-quarter of one cup

GUACAMOLE
Lime juice, two tablespoons
Avocado, two medium-sized
Tomatoes, chopped fine, two tablespoons
Red onion, chopped fine, two tablespoons
Cilantro, chopped fine, one tablespoon

Instructions:

Clean off the gills and stems from the Portobello mushrooms. Rinse off the mushroom caps and pat them dry. In a small-sized bowl cream together the cumin, harissa, onion powder, and one and one-half tablespoons of the olive oil until all ingredients are creamy and smooth. Completely cover the underside of each of the mushroom caps with this mixture, making sure to cover the edges too. Let them sit and marinate for fifteen minutes. Mix up the ingredients for the guacamole while you are letting the mushrooms marinade. After wiping off, the avocados cut them in half and use a spoon to scoop out the flesh. Put the flesh into a medium-sized bowl and stir in the lime juice, cilantro, red onion, and the chopped tomatoes. Rinse and dry the leaves of the collard greens and cut off the tough stems. When the mushrooms have finished marinating, put the remainder of the olive oil in a large skillet over a medium-high heat and let it get hot. Put the mushroom caps in the hot oil and fry them for three minutes on each side. Take the mushrooms from the oil and lay them on a paper-towel-lined plate. Let the mushrooms rest for five minutes before you slice them. Lay a few slices of the mushroom cap in a collard leaf. Top the slices with the guacamole and enjoy.

Nutrition info per two collards: Calories 405, 16 grams carbs, 35 grams fat, 10 grams protein

Egg Roll in a Bowl

Prep five min/cook fifteen min/serves two

Keto, low-carb, vegetarian, vegan

Ingredients:

Olive oil, one tablespoon
Black pepper, one teaspoon
Tamari, two tablespoons
Cabbage, four cups shredded
Sesame seeds, one-quarter of one cup for garnish
Carrots, two shredded to make one cup
Sesame oil, one teaspoon
Green onions, chopped, one half of one cup for garnish
Onion, red, one half sliced thin
Mushrooms, one cup sliced

Instructions:

Set a large-sized skillet on the stove over a medium-high heat and warm up the olive oil. Fry the carrots, celery, and onions for five minutes. Pour in the tamari, pepper, mushrooms, and shredded cabbage. Stir all these ingredients together well. Turn the heat down to low under the pan and let the mix simmer for fifteen minutes. Stir in the sesame oil for one minute and then take the pan off of the heat. Serve with the sesame seeds and the chopped green onions for garnish.

Nutrition info per serving: Calories 178, 12 grams carbs, 6 grams protein, 9 grams fat

Feta Chicken Pasta

Prep five min/cook thirty min/serves four

General diet

Ingredients:

Basil, fresh, fine chopped for garnish
Olive oil, two tablespoons
Feta cheese, four ounces divide
Black pepper, one half teaspoon
Whole wheat fettuccine, one pound
Diced tomatoes, two fourteen ounce cans with spices
Water, two cups
Chicken breast, two pounds cooked skinless and boneless, cut into chunks

Instructions:

Cook the chunks of the chicken breast in hot olive oil in a large pot for ten minutes, stirring often to cook all sides of chicken. Sprinkle on half of the pepper while stirring. Pour in the water and the diced tomatoes. Break the pasta in half and stir the pieces in, cooking them for ten minutes. Stir in one half of the feta cheese and cook this mixture for five more minutes. Garnish with the fresh basil and the other half of the feta cheese.

Nutrition: Calories 390, 11 grams fat, 56 grams carbs, 19 grams protein

Pigs in a Blanket

Prep twenty min/cook twenty min/serves six

Keto and low-carb

Ingredients:

Sesame seeds, one teaspoon
Hot dogs, all-beef, twelve
Onion powder, one teaspoon
Mozzarella cheese, shredded, two cups
Garlic powder, one half teaspoon
Eggs, two whisked
Oregano, dried, one teaspoon
Coconut flour, one half cup
Baking powder, one half teaspoon
Cream cheese, low fat, two ounces at room temperature

Instructions:

Heat the oven to 400. Lay parchment paper over a cookie sheet. Heat the cream cheese and mozzarella cheese in a heatproof bowl in the microwave for three minutes until they are softened, then mix the two cheeses together well until they are creamy. Use another bowl to mix together the eggs, garlic powder, baking powder, oregano, onion powder, and coconut flour until they are well mixed. Stir in the melted cheese to the dry mix after the cheese has cooled slightly. Wet your hands slightly and divide the dough into twelve equal-sized pieces and roll them into balls. Then roll the balls of dough out into circles where the width is the same as the hot dog is long. Roll up each hotdog with one circle of the dough and lay them on the parchment paper on the cookie sheet. Sprinkle the sesame seeds on the dough and then bake the dogs for twenty minutes until they are browned.

Nutrition per two dogs: Calories 370, 24 grams fat, 8 grams net carbs, 25 grams protein

Herbed Grilled Cod

Prep ten min/cook twenty min/serves four

Keto and low-carb

Ingredients:

Olive oil, two to four tablespoons
Cod fillets, eight pieces
Peppercorns, whole, one teaspoon
Turmeric, one teaspoon
Black pepper, one teaspoon
Rosemary, dried, one tablespoon
Dried fennel seeds, one teaspoon
Garlic, minced, two teaspoons
Thyme, dried, one tablespoon

Instructions:

Put the thyme, garlic, fennel seeds, rosemary, peppercorns, turmeric, and the black pepper into a small bowl and mix them together well. Coat both sides of the cod fillets with the olive oil. Press the cod fillets gently but deeply into the bowl of seasonings to coat both sides very well. Put the fillets on a plate and cover them and let them chill in the refrigerator for two hours. Cook the cod fillets under the broiler, five inches below the coils, or grill them on an outdoor grill for eight minutes on each side. Serve with a salad of fresh greens.

Nutrition: Calories 275, 17 grams fat, 1 gram carbs, 1 gram protein

Shrimp with Lemon and Garlic Pasta

Prep ten min/cook twenty min/serves four

General diet

Ingredients:

Jumbo shrimp, one pound peeled and deveined
Zucchini, two cups sliced thin
Grape tomatoes, one cup cut in halves
Parsley, chopped, one tablespoon
Garlic, minced, one tablespoon
Whole grain pasta any style, eight ounces
Red pepper flakes, one quarter teaspoon
Olive oil, three tablespoons
Lemon zest, one tablespoon
Black pepper, one half teaspoon
Lemon juice, two tablespoons
Instructions:

Cook the pasta per the package directions. While the pasta is cooking, cook the zucchini with the pepper for five minutes. Mix in the tomatoes and cook for three more minutes. Stir in the shrimp, red pepper flakes, and garlic and mix well. Cook this mixture for five minutes, stirring often, until the shrimp is done The shrimp will be pink when it is completely cooked. Stir the shrimp mix into the drained cooked pasta and mix well.

Nutrition info: Calories 474, 46 grams carbs, 15 grams fat, 37 grams protein

Mustard Crusted Salmon Fillets with Roast Cauliflower

Prep ten min/cook forty min/serves four

Keto and low-carb

Ingredients:

Salmon fillets, four six-ounce each
Olive oil, two tablespoons
Dijon mustard, three tablespoons
Cauliflower, six cups florets
Fresh dill, chopped, two teaspoons
Lemon juice, two teaspoons
Rosemary, one teaspoon

Black pepper, one teaspoon

Instructions:

Heat the oven to 400 degrees. Bake the cauliflower florets on a baking pan for twenty-five minutes. In a small bowl mix well the mustard, dill, and the lemon juice. Put the salmon fillets with the skin side down on a foil-covered baking pan and season them with the rosemary and the black pepper. Cover the fillets with the mustard mix and bake them for an additional fifteen minutes.

Nutrition: Calories 305, 12 grams fat, 10 grams carbs, 37 grams protein

Indian Roasted Vegetables

Prep ten min/cook twenty min/serves four

Keto, low-carb, vegetarian, vegan

Ingredients:

GARNISH
Green onion, diced, one half of one cup
Cilantro, chopped, one-quarter of one cup

VEGGIES
Green beans, three-fourths of one cup
Mushrooms, sliced, one half of one cup
Cauliflower, one cup in small pieces

MASALA SEASONING
Turmeric, one quarter teaspoon

114

Garlic, minced, one tablespoon
Black pepper, one half teaspoon
Tomato puree, one half of one cup
Olive oil, two tablespoons
Chili powder, ground, one half teaspoon
Ginger, ground, two teaspoons
Garam masala, one quarter teaspoon

Instructions:

Heat the oven to 400 and set the oven rack in the middle of the oven. Use olive oil spray to spray oil a cookie sheet. If the veggies have not been chopped, then chop them now. In a medium-sized mixing bowl, blend well together the garam masala, chili powder, garlic, ginger, pepper, and the tomato puree until all of the ingredients are mixed well together. Blend in the olive oil. Put the chopped veggies into this mix and stir them around until all of the veggies are covered well. Lay the veggies out on the cookie sheet in a single layer. Put the cookie sheet in the oven and roast the veggies for twenty to thirty minutes or until the veggies are cooked the way you like them.

Nutrition: Calories 105, 10 grams carbs, 7 grams fat, 3 grams protein

Cauliflower Pie

Prep thirty min/cook thirty min/serves four

Low-carb, vegetarian, vegan

Ingredients:
Balsamic vinegar, one fourth cup
Vegetable broth, one cup

Black pepper, one teaspoon
Tomato paste, one tablespoon
Carrots, two medium-sized peeled and diced fine
Thyme, dried, one teaspoon
Nutmeg, ground, one teaspoon
Cauliflower, one head
Onion, one medium-sized diced finely
Celery, one stalk washed and diced fine
Olive oil, two tablespoons
Dijon mustard, one tablespoon
Nutritional yeast, three tablespoons
Garlic, minced, three tablespoons
Mushrooms, diced small, one cup

Instructions:

Heat the oven to 400. Boil the cauliflower covered in water and cook for eight to ten minutes or until the pieces of cauliflower are very tender. Drain the water off and put the cauliflower into a medium-sized bowl and set it to the side. Set a large-sized skillet on the stove over medium-high heat. Warm the olive oil and pour in the carrots, celery, and onion. Cook these for five minutes, stirring occasionally. Pour in the diced mushroom and cook for another five minutes. Blend in the balsamic vinegar and the tomato paste. Cook for two minutes and then stir in the vegetable broth. Then simmer this mix for ten minutes or at least until around half of the liquid has been absorbed. While this mix is cooking, mash the cooked cauliflower. When the cauliflower is well-mashed, add in the thyme, mustard, pepper, nutmeg, and nutritional yeast. Pour the veggie mix into a square nine by nine-inch casserole dish and top with the mashed cauliflower mixture. Bake the casserole for twenty minutes.

Nutrition: Calories 400, 11 grams protein, 15 grams carbs, 15 grams fat

Roast Brussel Sprouts with Red Pepper and Garlic

Prep ten min/cook twenty min/serves four

Keto, low-carb, vegetarian, vegan

Ingredients:

Red pepper, crushed, one half teaspoon
Garlic, minced, two tablespoons
Black pepper, one teaspoon
Olive oil, four tablespoons divided
Brussel sprouts, two pounds

Instructions:

Heat the oven to 500. Trim off the bottom stems from the Brussel sprouts and put them into a medium-sized mixing bowl with the black pepper and two tablespoons of the olive oil. Toss the sprouts gently until all are well covered. Spread the oiled Brussel sprouts out onto a cookie sheet and cover them over with a sheet of foil. Bake the sprouts for ten minutes and take off the sheet of foil. Bake the Brussel sprouts for another ten minutes. While they are in the oven, put the remaining two tablespoons of olive oil into a medium-sized skillet and fry the crushed red pepper and the minced garlic together for three minutes. When the Brussel sprouts have finished cooking, mix them together with the fried garlic and red peppers, and serve.

Nutrition: Calories 195, 15 grams fat, 8 grams carbs, 6 grams protein

Veggie Salad Bowl

Prep thirty min/cook twenty min/serves four

Keto, low-carb, vegetarian, vegan

Ingredients:

VINAIGRETTE
Olive oil, three tablespoons
Apple cider vinegar, two tablespoons
Dijon mustard, two teaspoons
Black pepper, one teaspoon

SALAD
Zucchini, one small

Asparagus, one large bunch
Olive oil, two tablespoons
Walnuts, one-quarter of one cup
Avocado, one cubed
Spinach, fresh, two cups packed
Bell pepper, red, one medium
Purple cabbage, shredded, one half cup
Celery, two stalks diced
Parsley leaves, one half of one cup packed
Lettuce, mixed leaves, two cups packed

Instructions:

Heat the oven to 400. Peel off the skin of the zucchini and cut off the ends, and then cut the zucchini into long strips and cut them into diagonal pieces about one-half-inch thick. Wash and clean the bell pepper and cut it into slices. Clean the asparagus. Place all of the veggies into a medium-sized bowl and cover them with the olive oil. Mix the veggies together well until all of the pieces are well coated. Put the veggies in a single layer on a cookie sheet. Cook the veggies for twenty minutes. While the veggies are baking mix together all of the ingredients for the dressing in a small bowl. When the veggies are done, baking divide them evenly between four bowls and drizzle the mixed dressing over all of them and serve the salad immediately.

Nutrition: Calories 313, 5 grams carbs, 5 grams protein, 30 grams fat.

Zucchini Ravioli

Prep twenty five min/cook thirty five min/serves six

Low-carb, vegetarian, vegan

Ingredients:

TOPPING
Marinara sauce, one large jar

PINE NUT HEMP PARMESAN
Pine nuts, one fourth cup
Hemp seeds, one fourth cup

ZUCCHINI
Zucchini, four medium-sized
Basil, fresh, one cup
Water, one cup
Black pepper, one half teaspoon
Walnuts, one cup
Cashews, raw, one cup
Spinach, fresh, one cup
Garlic, minced, three tablespoons

Instructions:

Heat the oven to 350. Mix the ingredients for the pine nut hemp parmesan in a medium-sized bowl and grind them together with a pestle or use a food processor until they are crumbly. Wipe off and peel the zucchini and slice them in very thin strips from one end to another. You should be able to make thirteen to fifteen strips from one zucchini. Lay the slices of zucchini out on a paper towel not overlapping and sprinkle them with a bit of salt. Mix together the pepper, garlic, water, spinach, walnuts, basil, and cashews until all of these ingredients are mixed well. Grind these ingredients well with a pestle or in a food processor until they are almost pureed but still rather chunky. The salted zucchini strips will now have water drawn out of them by the salt, so wipe it off with a paper towel. Place two of the slices of zucchini on a plate in an 'X' shape. Drop a spoonful of the nutty ricotta mixture in the middle of the X. Take the ends of the strips and bring them all to the middle to make a small pocket. Put each of the ricotta-filled pockets into a nine by thirteen inch baking pan. When you have assembled all of the raviolis and placed them in the baking dish, then cover them with the marinara sauce. Sprinkle the pine nut hemp parmesan on top of the marinara. Bake the casserole for forty-five minutes and let it stand for ten minutes before serving. This recipe will make thirty raviolis, and one serving is five ravioli.

Nutrition info per five raviolis: Calories 360, 30 grams fat, 15 grams carbs, 12 grams protein

Beef and Blue Cheese Penne with Pesto

Prep ten min/cook twenty min/serves four

Keto

Ingredients:

Gorgonzola cheese, one-fourth cup crumbled
Black pepper, one half teaspoon
Walnuts, one-fourth cup chopped
Baby spinach, fresh, six cups coarsely chopped
Pesto, already prepared, one third cup
Grape tomatoes, two cups halved
Beef tenderloin steaks, two, six ounces each
Penne pasta, whole wheat, two cups cooked per package directions

Instructions:

While pasta is cooking broil the steaks five inches from heat for seven minutes on each side. After pasta is cooked drain it and place the pasta in a large bowl. Stir in the pesto, tomatoes, walnuts, and spinach and mix together well. Slice the steaks into quarter-inch thick slices and toss the slices with the pasta. Garnish with the cheese and serve.

Nutrition: Calories 532, 22 grams fat, 49 grams carbs, 35 grams protein.

Pepper Ricotta Primavera

Prep thirty min/serves six

Vegetarian and vegan

Ingredients:

Fettucine, whole wheat, six ounces cooked and drained
Almond milk, one half cup
Ricotta cheese, part-skim, one cup
Basil, dried, one fourth teaspoon
Sweet yellow pepper, one medium cut in julienne strips
Garlic, minced, one tablespoon
Oregano, dried, one fourth teaspoon
Peas, frozen, one cup thawed
Zucchini, one medium sliced thin
Olive oil, four tablespoons
Sweet red pepper, one medium cut in julienne strips
Red pepper flakes, crushed, one fourth teaspoon

Instructions:

Blend the almond milk and ricotta cheese and set to the side. Cook pepper flakes and garlic in the hot olive oil for two minutes. Stir in the oregano, zucchini, sweet peppers, peas, and basil and cook for five minutes. Pour the cheese mix over the fettuccine; add vegetables from skillet and toss well.

Nutrition info for one cup: Calories 229, 7 grams fat, 31 grams carbs, 11 grams protein.

Beef and Avocado Burger

Prep five min/cook fifteen min/serves one

Keto and low-carb

Ingredients:

Pepper, one half teaspoon
Ground beef, ninety percent lean, six ounces
Avocado, one-quarter medium sliced thin
Oregano, dried, one quarter teaspoon
Mustard, yellow or whole grain, one teaspoon

Instructions:

Use the pepper and oregano to season the beef and then shape it into a patty. Fry the burger patty for five minutes on each side, or until it is cooked to your preference. Spoon the mustard on top and then add the slices of avocado.

Nutrition: Calories 295, 4 grams carbs, 15 grams fat, 37 grams protein

Healthy Meatballs

Prep fifteen min/cook thirty min/serves four

Keto and low-carb

Ingredients:

Garlic, minced, two tablespoons
Lime juice, one tablespoon

Ground beef, two pounds
Cilantro, fresh chopped, one quarter cup
Ginger, ground, one half teaspoon

Instructions:

Heat the oven to 350. Use parchment paper or foil to cover a large cookie sheet. Put all of the ingredients together in a bowl and mix them well. Form the mix into twelve meatballs of about the same size. Set the meatballs on the cookie sheet and bake them for thirty minutes. Serve the meatballs with a side vegetable or a tossed salad.

Nutrition: Calories 288, 18 grams fat, 26 grams protein, 5 grams carbs

Chapter 8: Recipes For Snacks And Appetizers

Winter Fruit Salad

Ingredients:

DRESSING
Balsamic vinegar, one tablespoon
Olive oil, one tablespoon
Avocado oil, one tablespoon

SALAD
Persimmons, two cups of one-inch cubes, about four large persimmons
Pecan, slivered, three quarters cup
Pears, cut into cubes, two cups
Grapes, any color, one cup cut into halves

Instructions:

Mix up the dressing and then set it off to the side so the flavors can mix while you put together the salad. Cut the persimmons, pears, and grapes into pieces roughly the same size and mix together in a bowl. Pour the dressing onto the fruit and mix it well together. When you are ready to serve the fruit salad add in the slivered pecans.

Smoked Salmon Feta Cheese Endive Bites

Ingredients:

Smoked salmon, one package
Endive, three heads
Feta Cheese, herbed, one package

Instructions:

Cut the ends off of the bunches of the endive and pull all the leaves off. Spread the leaves with the feta cheese. Lay a slice of salmon on top of the cheese and serve.

Loaded Hummus

Ingredients:

HUMMUS
Chickpeas, one fifteen ounce can drain and rinse
Black pepper, one teaspoon
Olive oil, three tablespoons
Tahini, two tablespoons
Lemon juice, one teaspoon
Garlic, minced, one tablespoon
Water, four tablespoons
Cumin, ground, one fourth teaspoon
Paprika, ground, one half teaspoon

TOPPINGS
Cilantro, fresh chop, two tablespoons
Sesame seeds, two tablespoons
Cucumber, chopped, one fourth cup
Red onion, chopped, one fourth cup
Cherry tomatoes, one fourth cup
Chickpeas, one-fourth cup, toasted crispy

Instructions:

Heat the oven to 400. Put one-quarter cup of the chickpeas in the oven and bake them for twenty-five minutes to make them toasted crispy. Place all of the ingredients that are for the hummus in a blender or a food processor and puree them until they are creamy and smooth. Put the hummus onto a platter for serving and arrange the cucumber, onion, and tomatoes on top of the hummus. Garnish the hummus with the sesame seeds, cilantro, and crispy chickpeas. Arrange crackers or chunks of pita for dipping.

Greek Yogurt Artichoke Spinach Dip

Ingredients:

Parmesan cheese, shredded, one third cup
Mozzarella cheese, shredded, two-thirds cup
Feta cheese, crumbled, one cup
Garlic, minced, two teaspoons
Greek yogurt, plain, one and one third cups
Artichoke hearts, one fourteen ounce can drained and chopped
Frozen spinach, thawed, one ten-ounce package

Instructions:

Heat the oven to 350. Spray oil an eight by eight-inch baking dish. Squeeze the thawed spinach until all of the excess liquid comes out. Gently mix everything together in a medium-sized mixing bowl. Pour this mix into the oiled baking dish and bake the dip for thirty minutes. Serve the dip hot with crackers, veggies, or chips.

Mediterranean Veggie Fritters

Ingredients:

Olive oil, three tablespoons for frying
Garlic, minced, two tablespoons
Onions, two, minced
Carrots, grated, one cup
Scallions, thin slices, one fourth cup
Cornstarch, one fourth cup
Egg, two
Beets, two medium shredded

Lemon juice, one half teaspoon
Turmeric, ground, one half teaspoon
Cumin, ground, two teaspoons
Parsley, chopped, two tablespoons
Black pepper, two teaspoons
Coriander, ground, one fourth teaspoon
Cornstarch, four tablespoons

Instructions:

Cook the garlic and the onion in the hot olive oil for three minutes, and then place all of this in a large-sized mixing bowl. Add in the cornstarch, lemon juice, parsley, coriander, black pepper, parsley, turmeric, cumin, beets, carrots, and scallions. Mix everything together well until all of the ingredients are blended completely. In another bowl make a thick paste by beating the four tablespoons of cornstarch and the eggs together. Add this paste to the veggie mix and stir together until all of the ingredients are well mixed. Spoon the batter by tablespoons into the hot oil and fry for three to five minutes on each side.

Greek Meatballs

Ingredients:

Olive oil, one tablespoon
Red onion, grated, one-fourth of one onion
Turkey breast, ground, sixteen ounces
Dill, ground, one fourth teaspoon
Feta cheese, one half cup
Black pepper, one fourth teaspoon
Oregano, dried, one teaspoon
Garlic powder, one half teaspoon

Instructions:

Turn on the broiler in the oven and place the rack five inches below the coils. Mix all ingredients together until they are all well mixed. Scoop about one and one-half tablespoons of mix and form it into the shape of a meatball. Place the meatballs on a spray oiled cookie sheet. Broil them for ten minutes.

Baby Potatoes with Olive Pesto

Ingredients:

Baby red potatoes, three pounds (about thirty-six)
Greek yogurt, low-fat, one half cup
Olive oil, six tablespoons divided
Garlic, minced, two tablespoons
Green olives, stuffed with pimiento, one and one half cups
Pine nuts, toasted, one half cup
Onion, chopped, one half cup

Instructions:

Heat the oven to 400. Wash the potatoes and dry them and then put them in a large-sized mixing bowl. Add two tablespoons of the olive oil and mix the potatoes with the oil very well. Use olive oil spray to spray oil a cookie sheet and put the potatoes on it, and then bake the potatoes for thirty minutes. While the potatoes are baking blend together the rest of the olive oil with the pine nuts, onion, garlic, and olives and chop everything together until it is well mixed. After the potatoes have cooled slice a thin slice off each bottom to allow them to sit upright. Slice two lines in the top of each potato, making a cross on them in the middle, and squeeze gently to open the cross. Use a teaspoon to fill each potato with the pesto mix and garnish with the Greek yogurt.

Herb Cheese Bread

Ingredients:

Cumin, ground, one half teaspoon
Cheddar cheese, shredded, three-fourths cup
Oregano, dried, one fourth teaspoon
Green onions, fine chop, one fourth cup
Garlic, two tablespoons minced
French bread, unsliced, one loaf
Butter, one-third cup softened to room temp
Red pepper flakes, one fourth teaspoon
Thyme, dried, one fourth teaspoon

Instructions:

Heat the oven to 400. Cut the loaf of bread in half from one end to the other end. Cook the minced garlic and the chopped green onions in the butter for three minutes, and then pour them into a bowl along with the butter. Mix in the thyme, red pepper flakes, oregano, and the cumin. Use a knife to spread this mix over the inside halves of the bread. Wrap each half of the bread loosely in aluminum foil and bake, with the inside of the bread facing up, for twenty five minutes.

Tomato Parmesan Rosemary Palmiers

Ingredients:

Egg, one beaten
Black pepper, one half teaspoon
Rosemary, dried, one tablespoon
Parmesan cheese, grated, one fourth cup
Tomatoes, fine chop, one half cup
Puff pastry, one sheet ready-rolled

Instructions:

Heat the oven to 400. Put the sheet of puff pastry on a lightly floured counter or board and cover it with the rosemary, parmesan, pepper, and tomatoes. Roll the long sides of the pastry and make them meet in the middle. Use a pastry brush to coat the two sides with the beaten egg and then push the two sides together to make them stick to each other. Use an olive oil spray to spray oil one cookie sheet. Carefully slice the roll into one inch thick slices and lay the slices on the cookie sheet. Bake the palmiers for fifteen minutes.

Soy Yogurt Spinach Artichoke Dip

Ingredients:

Artichoke hearts, one can fourteen-ounce size drained and chopped small
Spinach, thawed from frozen, one ten-ounce package
Garlic, minced, two teaspoons
Soy yogurt, plain, one cup
Nutritional yeast, one half of one cup

Instructions:

Heat the oven to 350. Use olive oil spray oil to grease an eight by eight-inch baking pan. Squeeze the thawed spinach in between several layers of paper towels until all of the water is drained out. Mix together all of these ingredients and pour them into the oiled baking dish. Bake the dip for thirty minutes and serve it hot with vegan chips.

Avocado Cucumber Bites

Ingredients:

Cucumber, one medium-sized
Avocado, one large, peeled and pitted
Lime juice, one half teaspoon
Chives, chopped, one-quarter of one cup

Instructions:

Peel the cucumber if you prefer it to be peeled and then slice it into slices that are about one half of one inch thick. Lay the slices of cucumber on a plate. Mash the peeled avocado and then mix in the lime juice. Set one teaspoon of mashed avocado on top of each of the cucumber slices. Sprinkle the chopped chives on the top of the avocado.

Tuna Stuffed Avocados

Ingredients:

Basil, fresh sliced for garnish
Avocado, one large peeled
Black pepper, one half teaspoon
Albacore tuna, one can drain
Black olives, minced, two tablespoons
Pesto, two tablespoons
Tomatoes, minced, two tablespoons

Instructions:

Cut the avocado in half the long ways and remove the seed and throw it away. Use a spoon to scrape out two

135

tablespoons of the flesh from each half. Place the scraped flesh in a medium-sized mixing bowl. Add in the pesto and the tuna and mash this well and mix everything all together. Next add in the olives, black pepper, and tomatoes and mix well. Spoon the mixture into the avocado shell and enjoy.

White Bean Artichoke Dip

Ingredients:

White beans, one fifteen ounce can, drained and rinsed
Garlic, minced, four tablespoons
Artichoke hearts, six ounces can marinated
Olive oil, two tablespoons
Basil, ground, two tablespoons
Cayenne pepper, one half teaspoon
Lemon juice, two tablespoons

Puree together in a blender the garlic, artichokes, and white beans (a food processor also works well for this). Then add in the cayenne pepper, lemon juice, basil, and the olive oil. Serve this dip with vegetable sticks or toasted pita bread chips.

Roasted Chickpeas

Ingredients:

Chickpeas, two fifteen ounce cans, drain and rinse
Black pepper, one half teaspoon
Olive oil, two tablespoons
Garlic powder, one half teaspoon
Red wine vinegar, two teaspoons
Oregano, dried, one teaspoon
Lemon juice, two teaspoons

Instructions:

Heat the oven to 425. Pour the chickpeas onto a cookie sheet that you have used olive oil spray on. Bake the chickpeas for ten minutes, and then stir them and bake them for another ten minutes. Blend the black pepper, olive oil, garlic powder, red wine vinegar, oregano, and the lemon juice very well in a medium-sized mixing bowl. After the chickpeas have baked the second time pour them into the bowl of this mix and toss them to coat all of them very well. Bake the chickpeas another ten minutes, then let them cool and eat.

Baked Root Veggies with Parsley Buttermilk Dip

Ingredients:

PARSLEY BUTTERMILK DIP
Greek yogurt, low fat, one seven-ounce container
Lemon zest, one teaspoon
Parsley, minced, two tablespoons
Buttermilk, six tablespoons
Garlic, minced, two tablespoons

ROOT VEGGIE CHIPS
Turnip, one medium
Cumin, ground, one half teaspoon
Parsnip, one large
Garlic powder, one teaspoon
Golden beet, one medium
Thyme, dried, one half teaspoon
Red beet, one medium
Olive oil, two tablespoons

Instructions:

Heat the oven to 400. Make the dip first by mixing all of the ingredients for the dip together, then cover the dip and refrigerate it until it is needed. Mix the garlic powder, thyme, cumin, and olive oil together in a medium-sized mixing bowl. Wash, dry, and peel the veggies and slice very thin. If you have a mandolin it would work very well for this. Using a pastry brush coat both sides of all of the veggies with the olive oil mix, then lay them on a rack that is placed on a cookie sheet. Bake the oiled chips for twenty minutes, or a bit longer if you feel it is needed, until they are lightly browned and crispy. Serve warm or cooled with the dip.

Chapter 9: Recipes For Sauces And Dressings

Italian Dressing

Ingredients:

Balsamic vinegar, one quarter cup
Garlic, minced, one tablespoon
Parsley, fresh chop, one tablespoon
Oregano, dried, one teaspoon
Black pepper, one quarter teaspoon
Olive oil, three fourths cup

Instructions:

Use a medium sized mixing bowl to place all of the ingredients into and mix well until all of the ingredients for the dressing are well blended. This dressing will store well in the refrigerator. If kept in an airtight jar it will keep for up to four days.

Pepper Sauce

This is a great sauce to use to flavor any type of cooked vegetables.

Ingredients:

Vegetable broth, one cup
Greek yogurt, one half cup
Cornstarch, one half teaspoon
Green peppercorns, two tablespoons

Olive oil, one tablespoon
White pepper, ground, one half teaspoon
Yellow onion, one half medium, diced fine
Black pepper, one half teaspoon

Fry the onion in the olive oil using for five minutes. Pour in the vegetable broth and mix well. Stir in the white pepper, green peppercorns, and black pepper with the yogurt and let this mix simmer for eight to ten minutes while still stirring constantly. Add in the cornstarch and stir well and then remove the pot from the heat.

White Cheese Sauce

This sauce is great when served on any hot vegetable, particularly on asparagus or green beans.

Ingredients:

Cream cheese, low fat, eight ounces
Greek yogurt, one cup
Butter, one cup
Mozzarella cheese, shredded, two cups

Instructions:

Combine the butter, cream cheese, and the yogurt and stir constantly to prevent burning or sticking while they soften and blend. When everything is mixed together, then add in the mozzarella cheese. Continue stirring constantly until the cheese is fully melted and well mixed in. This sauce will keep for no more than three days and just needs rewarming over low heat or in the microwave to use later.

arinara Sauce

Ingredients:

Tomato puree, three cups
Onion flakes, two teaspoons
Oregano, fine chop, two teaspoons
Thyme, fine chop, two teaspoons
Parsley, fine chop, two tablespoons
Balsamic vinegar, one tablespoon
Black pepper, one teaspoon
Olive oil, two tablespoons
Garlic, minced, one tablespoon

Instructions:

Put the olive oil, thyme, garlic, onion flakes, and oregano in a pot and mix well. Pour in the tomato puree and mix it with the seasonings until everything is smoothly blended. Turn the burner on to a low heat and stir in the pepper and the balsamic vinegar and then bring the mixture to a simmer. Remove the pot from the heat and completely mix in the parsley.

Creamy Alfredo

Ingredients:

Olive oil, two tablespoons
White pepper, one quarter teaspoon
Parmesan cheese, fresh grated, two ounces
Nutmeg, ground, one quarter teaspoon
Egg, one
Greek yogurt, one cup
Cream cheese, three ounces at room temperature

Instructions:

Slowly melt the olive oil into the cream cheese over low heat. Stir often to mix them well. Stir in half of the yogurt and increase the heat slightly while stirring often until the mixture is hot. Stir in one half of the parmesan cheese and keep stirring frequently until it is melted. Add in the rest of the yogurt and the parmesan cheese and mix well. Crack the egg and drop it into a bowl and beat it well. When the cream and the cheese have been added and the sauce is hot pour in the egg while you are stirring the sauce continuously. Continue to cook the sauce and lower the heat while you are stirring frequently for about four to five minutes while the sauce begins to become thick. Add in the seasonings and stir well and serve.

Conclusion

Thank you for making it through to the end of Clean Eating Cookbook for Beginners: The Complete Clean Eating Book with Over 100 Healthy, Whole-Food Recipes for Instant, Overnight, and Easy Comfort Foods. Easy Keto, Low-Carb, Vegetarian, and Vegan Cookbook and Healthy Recipes for Weight Loss Diet by Courtney Fox, here's hope that it was informative and able to provide you with all of the tools you need to achieve your goals whatever they may be.

The next step is to totally revamp the way you have been eating all these years and start eating a clean diet. Once you have made the switch to the clean eating lifestyle you will experience a level of health and happiness that you have never felt before. And this is the book that will take you to that level, using the tips and recipes that you found inside.

Finally, if you found this book useful in any way, a review on Amazon is always appreciated!

48742180R00085